As a draughtsman and engraver Iain Macnab was a master, unique in his precision and economy of understatement, which was emotionly charged and lucidly expressed. His contribution to the British School of Engraving and its glorious history was a major one. As a Scotsman and Highlander his withering wit and relaxing humour led him either into trouble with his fellow artists or to sheer brilliance in the rendering of form. He was one of the most sought after teachers of his time and ran a private art school for a period of fifteen years, a record.

The comprehensive collection of works bound in this volume will give much pleasure and will speak for themselves. In the text Albert Garrett delves deeply into the worlds of drawing and engraving. He is an artist and engraver with a reputation extending to Canada, Switzerland and Monaco. His close friendship with Iain Macnab has resulted in a biography expressing the way an artist thinks and works. If the artist is very talented, his prevailing problem is to develop an intellectual agility capable of keeping his talent continuously taut.

There are five one man shows to his credit, and his reputation as an artist and engraver extends to Canada, Switzerland and Monaco. He is the President of The Society of Wood Engravers and Relief Printers and Chairman of Mall Prints Exhibitions (Federation of British Artists)

As a writer he is co-author of three books entitled "Colour in Architecture" 1967 and "Factory Building" 1967 (Leonard Hill) and "Physical Working Conditions" 1969 (Industrial Society). He was the art director for the film "Colour Today" 1961 (sponsors P.J.A.). His research experience includes "Colour in Motion" Automobile Engineer, 1962/3 (Colour of cars in relation to the accident rate). "Colour Stimulus" Building Materials 1967 (Colour schemes) and "Diagnostic colour from natural and artificial light sources in Dental Hospitals" 1973 a paper read at the Science Congress, Association Internationale de la Couleur, 73, at the University of York.

D1187595

WOOD ENGRAVINGS
AND DRAWINGS
OF
IAIN MACNAB of BARACHASTLAIN

WOOD ENGRAVINGS
AND DRAWINGS

OF

IAIN MACNAB of BARACHASTLAIN

by Albert Garrett

Published by

MIDAS BOOKS

12 DENE WAY · SPELDHURST · TUNBRIDGE WELLS · KENT TN3 0NX

© Albert Garrett 1973

ISBN 0 85936 011 3

Produced by PJH Graphic Services
Printed in England by George Pulman & Sons Limited

Preface

Iain Macnab of Barachastlain. P.R.O.I., R.E. was a remarkable person. He did not however cut off his ear or leave his wife for a moon and sixpence, neither for that matter did he provide works for critics to make moons of green cheese. He was a master engraver of the Twentieth Century print revolution, who loved life and left it richer than he found it.

For me he was a very good friend and councillor. In particular I owe him a great debt for the training he gave so freely in handling the affairs of artists and in the organising of exhibitions. From our long association I have benefited beyond measure from the experience of his qualitative judgement on aesthetics and I still retain the aim and hope to gain the wisdom he commanded, for which I must work.

As artists our ways and ages were different, but our views on fundamental principles were held in common. For this reason I wish for Iain to speak again, in the text on topics and values we so often discussed, in the belief that it will help others along the road to excellence. We both felt this quality, beyond price, was worth fighting for and we battled together to maintain these principles. With this quality of talent it is incumbent to help others. If vigilance is not kept, talents can be badly mauled; if fairness is not practised doors will close on imaginative effort. Meanness, always present as a line of least resistance withholds opportunity for others and has to be continuously fought against. This is because of the general flabbiness and dusty thinking which is all too common when a bunch of artists meet to organise their own world.

Frequently, many critical pundits, offer free of charge, peppered warnings and salty advice to artists who elect to write of others, and even worse, to write of friends. This is expressed in the two well known words "painter paint". To promulgate criticism, which should be analaysis, and work in aesthetics, which is really fundamental art research, is today, for the artist an heinous crime. The artist must conform to the size and scale of the image which happens to be reflected from their mirrors. We have both burnt our boats, written and published much, the more to be damned. We also had a sneaking admiration for the perspicacity of Edward Gordon Craig, who so brilliantly in so many fields, created an outsized and impossibly complex image, that he virtually became his own biographer. If he had waited for the writers of his time, he would have been almost lost. America is now supplying us with books on this very English artist, actor and writer.

We were both impatient at the outpourings of aesthetic smoke filtering through the time and space we shared. Most of the smoke arose from writers using private psychology as a literary crutch. Academically the discipline of psychology is now a disreputable one in our Universities, and those who represent the elite in this field, to whom we look for guidance, disagree among themselves on fundamental issues. Art criticism is still riddled with Freudian claptrap at a time when in the Universities those who read research papers on psychology to a scientific audience, need to go to great lengths to explain that their deductions about to be heard are free from the empirical Freudian concepts. Psychology has not moved far from its substitution for religion in this Century. Its influence on art is disruptive in form and a necessary ingredient in the cooking of content and meaning. The two fundamental disciplines mostly concerned with why we are here are art and science or science and art. These two forms of inquiry should be in balance and add up at any one time. We both believe in this concept. There are quite naturally those who hate the concept, but this is good and important that they do so, but to write at all one must perforce express a point of view. It is these differences of opinion which act as life's safety valve and ensure change and the sifting and modification of values.

Iain and I both disliked an ivory tower and the artists, architects and scientists who are so pure that retirement from life as it is, become inevitable. We have both touched and worked in tar and applied our work successfully to the commercial art publicity field and suffered no ill consequences. In fact, taking part in life as we found it was very important to us. As indeed was the professional status of the artist, which to say the least has suffered chronic corrosion and disintegration the like of which can only be compared with the opposite state of affairs which obtained in the previous century. At that time an art dealer rarely passed beyond the butler, today they do not even need to visit studios. We worked together trying to arrest the corroding image. Like psychology the art profession has become academically disreputable, which naturally leads to all the disrespect now being poured on the profession and business. But at the same time, art is more highly charged with creative energy than in many previous centuries. There is however some comfort in being at rock bottom, from that vantage point reconstruction can commence.

The important thing about Iain is his work and its relationship to the time in which he lived and the significance of his contribution to our history. The intrinsic value of the work of an artist of Iain's quality cannot be measured in market values. It represents an unsolicited gesture of open generosity, expressing faith in man and the future and an unquestioning love of life, given freely with no hope of adequate reward, and with no view other than, he found he had such talent, and would have broken faith with his Creator, had he not used it.

The exciting aspect of this book is the reality of seeing a collection of his works, under one cover in the peace of our own homes. Iain was always concerned about communication and the spectator's point of view, an unusual one perhaps for the present time, but still relevant and professional. He said "If a drawing is a rhythmic organisation of forms, based on and symbolising the human figure and so composed and created that it evokes in us sensations similar to those experienced by the artist, and again if we find that these sensations are of interest to us aesthetically, we agree that it is a good drawing".

For a work of art to be complete three requirements need to be satisfied; one, the artist must have an aesthetic idea significant enough to make the requirement; two, the idea must be expressed in the form of an actual work; and three, there must be at least one other observer who understands what is being said. Then once a work of art always a work of art.

Contents

LIST OF ILLUSTRATIONS

WOOD ENGRAVINGS

DRAWINGS

Foreword

by

Brigadier John Francis Macnab of Barravorich CBE, DSO.

Iain Macnab of Barachastlain, as you will read further in this book, was, like most Highlanders a romanticist about all matters highland and took a great pride in the fact that there had been an artist-craftsman in every succeeding generation for certainly over four hundred years, and most probably for longer, in his family.

Of the eight cadet houses of the Clan Macnab Barachastlain is the fourth senior immediately preceeded by Barravorich. My much valued friendship with Iain began through our mutual interest in Clan Macnab affairs. We both became Representers of our respective Cadet houses about the same time and our Arms were matriculated within a few years of each other. We found that our two houses were the only two cadet families situated in Argyll within some twenty miles of each other and that our ancestors were at the battle of Waterloo together and also met in Canada in the nineteenth century.

Barachastlain is situated on the hill behind the present Dalmally hotel, not far from the southern end of beautiful and wild Glen Orchy. There is nothing left but a few ruins, as the stones were removed to make shelters for the navvies making the Highland railway. (A fate shared by Barravorich at the northern end of Glen Orchy and on the old drovers road to Loch Rannoch beside the water of Tulla on the edge of the moor of Rannock). We spent some memorable days together visiting the sites where our forebears lived and I have a water colour painted by Iain of the view from Barravorich looking west. I remember being astonished by the speed with which he completed this delightful picture: bringing in the swing of the dark clouds moving south which forced him to take cover from time to time from intermittent showers. These days went all too quickly and nightfall would find us, such was our enthusiasm, still looking at gravestones by the light of a torch; generally in a drizzle. Anyone visiting Loch Awe side after passing through Dalmally may see an engraved tablet to Iain's memory in the chancel of St. Conan's Kirk a few miles from Barachastlain and the country he loved so well.

Iain was to have sat his finals in chartered accountancy in October 1914. He told me much against his will, for he had always wanted to be a full time artist. The Kaiser's War brought release from his studies for he joined up in the Glasgow Highlanders as a Jock and was in one of the first drafts to France in August 1914, incidentally only being issued with a rifle at Dover. He fought at Mons and was sent shortly afterwards to the officers' training establishment at Bailloul behind the line. He was commissioned into the 2nd Battalion The Argyll and Sutherland Highlanders, and the 93rd Highlanders and served with them until 1916 when he was invalided out after being blown up at the battle of Loos.

On return to Britain he studied at the Glasgow School of Art — Heatherly in London and later in Paris. As you will read later his Barachastlain forebears were armourers. With Iain's invariable modesty he insisted that his skill as an engraver was inherited and directly attributable to his Highland ancestors. He dearly wanted to be a sculptor but unfortunately his war wounds precluded this. These did not, however, stop him from serving as an Air Raid Warden during the blitz on London in World War 2. Later he joined the Royal Air Force and served until 1944 when he was again invalided out.

In 1955 I managed to inveigle Iain to come and stay with us in Kenya during the later stages of the Mau Mau rebellion when at the age of 65 he held an exhibition of some fifty pictures executed in two months. He climbed to 10,000 feet on Mount Kenya and did some charcoal drawings of Kings African Rifles "Askari" in the bamboo forest. In addition he managed to help a young schoolmaster who is now a highly successful artist.

To know Iain was a great privilege and I am sure that this book will be much welcomed by his many friends, whether Artists, or just ungifted friends; so many of whom admired and loved him for his qualities of kindliness, generosity and humour.

Acknowledgements

The task of recreating an artist's life using words can only be done through the help of other people and in particular by those who knew Iain. My most sincere thanks are due to Helen Macnab, F.I.S.T.D. for supplying me so freely with the larger body of information and for the time and patience she gave to the task of detail and reading the manuscript.

Iain's personal friends made a very generous contribution to this work and my grateful thanks and appreciation are extended to Brigadier John Francis Macnab of Barravorich, C.B.E., D.S.O., Guy Malet R.B.A., Gwenda Morgan R.E., Maurice Bradshaw F.R.S.A., George Mackley R.E. and Ernest Fedarb. The colour they provided was invaluable. Further material was also provided and generously given by Kenneth Lindley A.R.E., A.T.D., M.I.S.A., Malcom Fry H.R.W.S., F.R.S.A., Sybella Stiles and Tom M. Doust A.L.A. I wish to thank them for their good will in helping to make this book a true record.

The recording of historical facts and quotations, so vital in determining time and place, would not have been possible without the help of the many authors, editors and publishers and I wish to thank James Lansdale Hodson for "No phantoms here" and the publisher Faber and Faber, and the Editors of the Observer for their micro film projection of the 1936 letter, The Architect, Jewish Guardian, Sunday Times, The Birmingham Gazette, The Yorkshire Post, The Guardian and the publishers Penguin Books Ltd., The Studio Ltd., Sir Isaac Pitman, David and Charles and the Artist Pub. Co. Ltd. My thanks are also due to The Arts Council for the quotation from Bernard Meninsky.

1 - Born a Scotsman

Iain had the most lovable quality of appearing to people and his friends as they wished to know him. He was an entertaining personality and it was always a pleasure to be in his company. Iain was the sort of man whom you would go to see for half an hour and find yourself still talking three hours later. Many knew only one facet of the whole person, some would get to know, perhaps two or more facets. But few enjoyed the experience of knowing the complete diamond. Many artists knew him as a painter, but not as an engraver, some knew him as an engraver, but not as a draughtsman and others knew him as a teacher and organiser, but not his work. Some artists in their maturity became pompous and pontifical bores and these were always good game for Iain's wit, which he would direct through understatement at their closely guarded but insecure underpinning. In many a committee meeting he would throw a carrot to a pompous bore for him to chew from bottom to top and thereby lose the vote to Iain's cause. Iain's timing was always accurate on these ocassions. There was nothing he loved more than to see two artists having a row over hanging pictures at an exhibition. A notorious pair who could always be relied upon for this type of entertainment at the Royal Institute of Oil Painters exhibitions were the late Bill Adams (English) and the late Stanley Grimm (Russian), both typical Chelsea pontiffs. He would let the fight continue and enjoy the fun, then quietly walk in and give a decision and leave them to lick their wounds. An important part of Iain's character was his ability to add up, not only people, but sums as well. Devilment often landed him in trouble but his sense of humour usually got him free.

Iain was not cast as in a mould, and because of this characteristic his image would fit no ready made mould and in art there are many ready made moulds, some deceptively attractive for those who are prepared to trim to fit. He was sharply chiselled in features with a face square in form and faceted as the light beam, many times reflected and refracted, determining in its travels, the crystal cut form of the gem. The form of the face confirmed the depth of the diamond. A diamond's truth is the authority of the geometric unity between the totally internally refracted beam and the outer form arising in consequence. The beam is trapped inside the diamond. Iain was a personality of great depths, where the inner reflected the outer man. He wore his art and authority as lightly as a mantle, with the sparkle of the diamond and his nonchalance was disarming, yet it was a protection device, used to protect the light beam inside the form. He would laugh at adversity, devalue success and power. Those not knowing the structure of the diamond would be content with the effect. He was of medium build, appeared sturdy even when he was far from it and allowed his hair, moustache, and trim distinctive beard to grow its natural way and the trimness and lively blue eyes gave him something of the appearance of the soldier having a day off. He was nevertheless a complete artist.

His many friends and acquaintances were largely orientated in the many aspects of the art sphere and facet would meet facet and stimulate communication, whether in painting, drawing, engraving, design, history, teaching, writing or organising exhibitions and people. In all these branches of art he was well known in his life time. To each he would talk shop in their own particular sphere. It was not that his talents were so wide, it meant that his versatility was flexible and accurate and he was able to direct his art into many channels and his intellect thereby was continually keeping his talent taut. This was what Iain wanted and art for him meant living it as well as producing it. For art to thrive its focus must be trained on something outside of and greater than the artist.

For the purpose of living the art, he would in his lighter moods, transfer this concept into more tangible terms. On receiving an invitation to visit him at 33 Warwick Square it was important to know something about whisky first, sherry second and thirdly wine. At 33 Warwick Square there was more than one door upon which a visitor could knock. But Iain would always insist that every visitor would enter on his first visit by the front door in the Scottish tradition. To fail in the appreciation of these three drinks and sometimes rare blends, could land the visitor as an emperor without clothes. His unwillingness to conform cut across today's pattern for worldly success which virtually demands that an artist must be either a painter, engraver or sculptor. He would also rarely attempt to interest a painter in engraving, especially if he knew beforehand that his listener had no background in this form of expression. The same would apply equally to an engraver or print artist who had no background in painting and so on throughout his range of subjects and circle of friends. This reflection illustrates just how close artists are to their reflected public image which is mirrored through the publicity channels. We have arrived at a stage in publicity where the personality is required to fit in the pocket. It was not until recent history that an artist was naturally expected to work in painting or sculpture and a print medium. For no other reason than a print medium enables the artist to develop his means of drawing expression. This should apply to all print media and the attending multiplying of the image by the print is or should be quite incidental.

Iain's image in the press also followed the disjointed faceted pattern over his life span. Most exhibitions and events are organised to promote one thing only, such as painting, drawing or prints as the case may be. The same pattern obtains also with art dealers and private galleries. It is the selling pattern which stems from the public's buying interests and this influences many artists much more than they are sometimes prepared to admit. Because of this selling structure Iain's work would appear in a large number of exhibitions in different parts of this country and overseas and covering a wide field of expression. Each year a crop of newspaper cuttings would appear as critical buckshot patterns now so useful in art history research. This critical buckshot does however add up to one clear consistent statement, which was, Iain's work was widely known and accepted as good and that he was an important artist. And this monotonous but happy song went on year after year. From this picture we do know that the artist has a wide public and it naturally lead to a large collector following in many countries. Today this would be referred to as International status, but that can be hollow and over done. But all this critical buckshot gave no indication of what the complete artist was really like, yet alone his breadth.

Much of Iain's personality and character can only be explained by the fact that he was a Scotsman. Born in 1890 on an island in the Philippines, called Iloilo. His father, John Macnab was with the Hong Kong & Shanghai Bank and worked as manager in many branches in the Far East. The Philippines were then Spanish possessions and Iain spoke Spanish before he learnt English, as his parents did not want him to have a foreign accent. The only English he learned as a child came through the unsatisfactory efforts of his Chinese amah. He came to Scotland when he was four years of age and was brought up in Kilmacolm. Later he was to spend some time caricaturing his teachers. Iain used to love to relate the story of his art master at the Merchiston School, Edinburgh. He told his master that his drawing and teaching method was all wrong. The master briskly turfed him out of his room by the scruff of his neck, with a curt "Get out". Iain would say that he was right about the method, but the master was right to throw him out. In those days in those schools art teaching did not go very far beyond the misdirected copying. The same art master at Merchiston promised him the drawing prize, but later changed his mind and gave it to Iain Bartholomew of the map making family as the family had just bought one of his pictures and as a consolation to Mac said, "You may have one of my water-colours to copy". Iain made the somewhat precocious reply, "I would rather make my own mistakes, thank you". James Lansdale Hodson in his book "No phantoms here". 1932 records another excursion of Iain's youth, "On one occasion when a boy sailing his small yacht he stove in some planks of Ian Hay's boat moored nearby. In trepidation he went off to tell the great man (as he seemed to Iain), "I'm sorry but I've stove in your boat," he said. "You've what?" roared Hay, "I've stove in ..." the boy stopped. Laughter was glinting in Hay's eye. Macnab laughed; Hay laughed. But life wasn't always so easy.

Iain was eventually trained as a chartered accountant at Rattsy Brothers, Alexander and France approximately 1911 in Glasgow. He never had the slightest intention of sticking to it. This training however was to take him a very long way into the management of a considerable slice of London's art world.

At the appropriate time and place he would often lay great stress on the fact that he was a Highlander. This was very important, evidently there are two primary divisions amongst Scotsmen; the Highlanders and Lowlanders. The dividing line is vertical to the north and central from the border and not as many people assume central and horizontal. This division explains to some extent the differing relationships between Edinburgh the Lowland capital and Glasgow the Highland capital communities. The Highlanders evidently are tough fighters and very generous and hospitable. But should you be on the other side of the line, then you are just different or indifferent. In many respects this difference of temperament coloured parts of Iain's character and gave emphasis to his scale of values. He was throughout his life always a fighter who enjoyed the combat, and his generosity also led him into pet and very strong hates. One of his big hates was meanness in any form or kind. He eliminated it from his affairs and his work contains no trace of meanness. Perhaps the meanness he hated most was in people who were in a position to help others and being too lazy to do so. His temper was readily excitable and when roused by dumbness and or stupidity from people holding authority, he would give full expression to a conciseness of words, devoid of tact, and loaded with an acid wit. For a recipient to come under such fire was to say the least a withering experience.

Questions of loyalty spring from the subject of meanness, and a story he enjoyed to tell was related to a group of Scots warriors fighting on the losing side, but with the Sassennach, or English. On being captured they were disarmed and placed in the dungeons, then offered their freedom in return for useful information. The Scotsmen then gave the required information and promptly had their throats cut. This had a salutary effect upon Iain, in that all were suspect in loyalty until proven. Much of his thinking and action was related very closely to people, rather than academic theory, whether political, economic or academic. Many people react in a manner quite different from that so often projected by theory.

Iain lived most of his life in London as a voluntary exile. He chose this because as he said, "London is the art centre and it is important to compete in it." He also said, "Art in Scotland is too parochial and the Academies do not like those artists who seek their fortunes over the border." Knowing him gave me a valuable introduction into the fascinating and lively way Scotsmen live the Scottish life, regardless of what country they may dwell in. They relive their history and bring it into everyday affairs and preserve their native culture. I feel that we can learn some good lessons from this. It would appear that the emotions and devotions of winning and losing battles in the 14th or 15th centuries are preserved intact and even sewn up in the Scotsman before he is born. When Iain started talking about the Clan this was the time for an Englishman or Sassenach to just sit and listen, because a lot of feathers would be torn from the Imperial image and our character would be seen and commented upon from a different perspective with its vanishing point well over the border or eye level. On these occasions I learned to understand the depth of emotion and sense of history behind Iain's remark. "A Highlander is very generous and never forgives a hurt or enemy". In Macnab Clan life he was very active as a member of the London Branch and was also an Hon. Vice President of the Clan Macnab Society. He was recognised by the Lord Lyon as the head of the Barachastlain Branch of the Clan and as holding the rank of Hereditary Standard Bearer to the Macnab of Macnab.

In Whitakers Almanac the Court of the Lord Lyon reads as follows. "The list of Chiefs comprises the persons officially recognised as such by inheritance of the ancestral arms ' without brisur or mark of cadency ' under the Act 1672 cap. 47 and/or relative supporters, under decree of the Court of the Lord Lyon.... These broad based family organisations were termed ' Names ' in the Lowlands, where all members bore the same basic surname, and ' Clans ' in the Border and Highland areas where surnames were a later development and evolved from complicated genealogical descriptions, the ' clan name ' being normally the name of the chief's house." Such is the family structure and it is little wonder that the Highlanders and lowlanders can identify each other so easily.

The colours of the Macnab tartan are green, crimson and red. Made up in wool the colours are subtle and the full dress is very impressive. One cannot but feel a certain loss in the fact that we Sassennachs have never been able to create a national costume. In the heraldic bearings the Clan Macnab has a savage's head in the crest and a bramble in the badge. *Fig. 1.* The matriculations of the Arms of Macnab of Barachastalain took place the 5th day of November 1958. An extract from the 9th page of the XLIIIrd Volume of the Public Register of all Arms and Bearings in Scotland gives the following information. Iain Macnab of Barachastalain, Captain late 2nd Battalion Princess Louise's Argyll and Sutherland Highlanders, Vice-President of the Royal Institute of Painters in Oils, residing at 33 Warwick Square, Westminster, London, S.W.1., having by Petition unto the Lord Lyon King of Arms of date 12th March 1958 shewn: that the Petitioner, born 21st October 1890 in the Philippine Islands (who married Helen Mary daughter of Rowland Tench, High Sheriff of Radnorshire) is the eldest son (his brother Alexander, born 1899, died of wounds 1918, and his brother Hector Archibald, born 1901, married Mary Rhona Mackinnon, and has with other issue a son Alastair Iain, Pilot Officer, R.A.F.) of John Macnab of the Hong Kong and Shanghai Bank and his wife Jessie Mabel daughter of Peter Shannan, Architect; that the Petitioner's said father, born 1847 and died 1927, was the only son of Alexander Macnab, Engineer, and his wife Mary daughter of Hugh Cowan, burgess of Oban; that the petitioner's said grandfather, born 1817 and drowned 1869 in Sydney, New South Wales, was the third son (but the eldest son John, born 1810, died young, and no issue of the second son, Peter, born 1812, now survive) of Donald Macnab, Builder in Oban, and his wife Catherine Sinclair; that the said Donald Macnab, born 1774, died 10 February 1850 and buried Muckairn Churchyard, Jaynuilt, was the son of Alexander Macnab, Merchant in Oban, an Elder of Glenorchy Kirk Session; which Alexander, born 1736 and died 19 August 1812, was third son (the eldest son Patrick Dow left an only son Alexander, died 1814, who left an only son, John who left no male issue, and the second

Figure 1 — *Iain's Book Plate.*

son Donald, died 1815, had three sons (1) John, born 1777, died without issue, (2) Robert, who served in the Army, later went to Canada and then to Tennessee, and of whom all trace was lost, (3) Duncan, born 1785 and died 1849, who as Deputy Commissary General went to Canada 1832 for the building of the Ripeau Canal and whose male issue expired on the death 1956 in Hawaii of his grandson Colonel Alexander James Macnab of the United States Army) of Donald Macnab and his first wife Mary Campbell; that in the Schedule of Branches of the House of Macnab of Macnab compiled by Archibald Macnab of Macnab, 17th Chief at Hamilton, Ontario, on 15th March 1847, the aforementioned Commissary General Duncan Macnab was recognised as Representer of Barachastalain, the ancient Armourers and Standard Bearers of the Chief now represented by Archibald Conie Macnab of Macnab and Kinnell whose Arms are recorded in the Public Register of all Arms and Bearings in Scotland (Volume XI page 133) of date 1st February 1956 and the fourth most ancient cadet of the Family of Macnab of Macnab; and the Petitioner having prayed that he might be recognised as Representer of Barachastalain and his Arms as such recorded in the said Public Register, The Lord Lyon King of Arms by Interlocutor of date 9th May 1958 Recognised the Petitioner as Chieftain of the House of Macnab of Barachastlain, and Granted Warrant to the Lyon Clerk to matriculate in the Public Register of all Arms and Bearings in Scotland in name of the Petitioner the following Ensigns — Armorial, videlicet:- Sable, on a chevron Argent three crescents Vert, in base an open boat, oars in action in a sea proper; a berdure Azure for difference; above the Shield is placed an Helm befitting his degree, with a mantling Sable doubled Argent, and on a Wreath of the Liveries is set for Crest a savage's head erased proper issuant from an armoured gorget also proper, and in an Escrol over the same this Motto BARR A' CHAISTEALAIN, and in an Escrol below the Shield this Motto EAGAL? CHA'N AITHNE OHOMH E!

The lands of the Macnab lay roughly on the border of the Highlands and Lowlands, which stretch from Loch Lomond, Loch Katrine to Loch Earn up to Loch Tay to the north. From the south it starts from Aberfoyle, Crainlarich, Bridge of Orchy and concluding at the north at

Fortingall. The Macnabs are usually referred to as an unfortunate fringe clan and did not share in the war-like exploits of their countrymen north of the Highland line. Early in the 14th century the clan was however raided by King Robert the Bruce and the lands were ravaged, houses burned and family papers destroyed. Only the barony of Bovain, in Glen Dockart was left to them. The Macnabs sided with the Macdougalls against Robert the Bruce as a result of the murder of the "Red Comyn".

During the reign of James IV the clan began to prosper and recover some of the strength lost in the time of King Robert the Bruce and a severe set-back hit them in 1552. Finlay the sixth chief of the clan, was compelled to mortgage the greater part of his estates to Campbell of Glenorchy: the Macnabs themselves would have no truck with Campbell, whom they recognised as ruler, but not owner of the lands. In 1552 the Macnabs engaged a deadly feud between Finlay the seventh chief and the Neishes who occupied part of Strathearn and a small island near the foot of Loch Earn. Skirmishes between the two were frequent, but in one decisive battle, the Macnabs cut down the Neishes almost to a man.

One day the Neishes made a terrible mistake. They captured Macnab's servant and robbed him. A grim Macnab heard the news in silence, his heart was afire with anger. His twelve sons, all strong and powerful men, thought of nothing but revenge. One evening Finlay addressed his sons in Gaelic "The night is the night, if the lads were but lads". On receiving this challenge each man sprang to his feet, belting on dirk, claymore and pistol. Led by John, they lifted a fishing boat from Loch Tay on to their shoulders, then carried it over the mountains to Loch Earn. A short row brought them to Neish Island, where they carried out a swift and terrible revenge. Every Neish excepting an old man and a boy was run through by the sword and their heads as trophies were taken back to the Macnab chief. The skirmishing however continued and having supported the Great Duke of Montrose the Macnab Castle at Dalmally, the northern tip of Loch Awe was razed to the ground. From then on the chiefs lived in Kinwell House, Killin in Perthshire, which had been the Dower House. They still do. The Neishes are now known as McInner.

Possibly the most famous and later chief of the clan was Francis Macnab of Macnab, a gigantic, swashbuckling character immortalised in Raeburn's portrait. Haughty, unbending and proud, he objected to what he called the usurpation of the Highlands by the unpedigreed. He placed himself well above the merchants and refused to pay their bills. These had to be paid in the end by the next in succession.

The burden of his debts fell on his nephew, Archibald, the thirteenth chief and the only solution he found was to flee to Canada. He bought some land with the intention of settling on it as many Macnab families as possible. The adventure failed and ended in suffering and appalling hardship. With Iain the 1552 skirmish of Macnab versus Neish of Loch Earn lived on. One day his wife said to him "You know I could have been born a Neish, what would you have done then?" To this remark Iain replied "I would not have been able to even meet you".

In 1936 the Macnab Clan made more news in the Observer. Their Ottawa Correspondent under the title 'Home of Famous Settler.' 'Deliberately destroyed', 'Sightseer's annoy descendant', writes;

"The century-old home of the Laid of Mc Nab, the Scottish chieftain who brought eighty-five clansmen to Canada in 1825 and settled on an 80,000 acre tract given them by the Government of Upper Canada, has been deliberately destroyed at Arnprior."

John Box, the Mc Nab descendant, who is the present resident on the land where the original Mc Nab home now stands, has knocked away the crumbling foundations and let the building collapse into a heap of debris.

Box explained that he and his mother had been "pestered to death by people asking questions about the building and by picnic parties who visited the grounds, trampled potato and corn crops, and often went away leaving fires after their picnics."

The Mc Nab, whose name has become a legend in eastern Ontario, was a giant of a man who ruled his clansman with a rod of iron, and sought to preserve feudalism in the new land.

The eighty-five settlers who came out with Mc Nab soon found their dream of becoming free men in a free land shattered when the chief forced them to pay tithes to him, perform services and do homage, although the land had been a free gift to the settlers from the Government of Upper Canada.

Mc Nab was finally brought before the court of Quarter Sessions at Perth, which was then capital of the district, and his career as a feudal chieftain was summarily checked. After fifteen years of misrule he left Canada and returned to Europe, and finally died in France in 1843, a broken man.

This article was followed by a letter written by Mr. T.H. Vale and reads, "The Clan Macnab".

Sir — I have read with regret your Ottawa Correspondent's account of the deliberate destruction of the Canadian home of the real recognised Macnab-chieftain.

I use the qualification 'recognised,' because since the death of the thirteenth chief — the subject of your article — who died childless, the chieftainship of the clan has been claimed by more than one descendant of the century Abbot or Prior of Glendochart, from whom the race took its subsequent name of Mac-an-Abbe or Mac Nab, the son of the abbot.

Upon the return of the disappointed and impoverished chieftain from Canada under circumstances related by your Correspondent, about 1840, he disposed of his last possession in this country, the Dreadnought Hotel at Callander, the forerunner of the present well-known hotel, which derives its name from the ancient clan motto, and which displays to this day over its doorway the cognisance of the Mac Nabs — the decapitated head of the clan Neish chieftain.

I wonder if amongst your readers there is a member of the clan Mac Nab with its septs of Abbot, Abbotson, Gilfillan and Dewar, who would enlighten me as to whether there is a recognised or acknowledged chief today.

The father of the emigrant chieftain, Francis, the twelfth chieftain of the Mac Nabs, who died in May, 1816 was a fantastic and picturesque figure in his day, and many anecdotes of his arbitrary and feudalistic character were related long after his death.

One story which I do not think appears in Lockhart's "Life of Sir Walter Scott" may be of interest to your readers.

Old Francis had necessity on one occasion to visit Glasgow on some business relating to his financial affairs, taking with him for "tail" one of his henchmen.

He put up at the Saracens Head Inn, and on the importance of the visit becoming known, he was accommodated with the "Chamber of Dais" the best bedroom. He found himself confronted, with a great fourposter bedstead, a contrivance with which he had not been hitherto acquainted. Looking at it for a moment and pointing to the bed itself, he said to his man, "Donald, get ye in there. The Mac Nab must go aloft", and with the aid of his henchman he clambered his way on to the canopy above.

After an hour of restless discomfort he called to his gillie, "Donald man. Are ye asleep?" The only reply was a happy snore from the fortunate henchman comfortably stretched on the feather bed below. "Donald ye rascal." he called again and having succeeded in arousing his man by repeated remonstrances he enquired, "Are ye comfortable doun there?" Donald said he was indeed verre comfortable, whereupon the Mac Nab rejoined, "Man if it were'na for the honour of the think I hae minds to come down and join ye."

A week later in the Observer 17th May, Iain followed with a letter coloured with Scottish wit and humour.

The Glorious Macnabs.

Sir — May I make a mild protest at the repetition by your correspondent Mr. Vale of the story of the chief of the clan and the fourposter bed, as from all accounts Francis Macnab of that ilk was a man of enterprise and resource?

In using his regiment, the Breadalbane Fencibles to escort smuggled brandy and in commanding them to fix bayonets and charge when three zealous but rash preventive officers tried to stop him, did he not show an intelligent anticipation of recent methods in America? When, another time, in London, he was challenged by an Englishman who owned a famous fighting cock, did he not confound the Sassennach (and win the wager of two thousand guineas) by bringing from Killin an enormous cock eagle, which had not been fed for days and which speedily devoured the other cock, spurs and all?

It is hardly probable that a gentleman of this character and of his station would be puzzled by a fourposter bed. No, as the old Highlandman, who told me the story of the cock fight many years ago, remarked cryptically, "We may pe Hielan' but were no so Hielan' as we look."

I would also point out that the Anglicised form of Mac-an-Abba is Macnab (sometimes Macnabb) and not Mac Nab as an extra capital would be more correctly used for the second A and not the N.

Answering Mr. Vale's question, no claimant has yet been able to substantiate his claim to the chieftainship. A pity, as according to legend, it is of such antiquity that we had our own boat at the time of the Flood.

33 Warwick Square, S.W.1.

The recently late chief was James Macnab — nephew of Archibald Macnab who died about 1969. During the late fifties Iain undertook some historical research into the lineage of his family and the Macnab Clan. The result makes very interesting reading. This work was first published in the Clan Macnab Society news letter in 1961, and the original version is published here.

THE HOUSE OF MACNAB OF BARACHASTLAIN
By Iain Macnab of Barachastlain

The Macnabs of Barachastlain, Hereditary Armourers and Standard Bearers of the Chiefs of the Clan, and fourth senior Cadets of the House of Macnab of Macnab, are one of the two Argyll Branches, the other being Barravorich, the third senior House. The Barachastlain Branch claim descent from Duncan the second son of Finlay II of Macnab. By the Charter restoring to his father the Barony of Bouvain, he is accounted only the second Chief although, according to the Gaelic genealogy of 1350, he was the twenty-second of his line.

Duncan was born either in 1400 or a year or two later. When his elder brother Patrick became Macnab of that Ilk on the death of his father, Duncan and his brothers had, in accordance with custom, to fend for themselves. Tradition says that having great natural skill in the handling of tools and metals and wishing to gain mastery of his chosen career, the making of swords and armour, Duncan set out for Italy.

A far cry from Glendochart! If tradition says true and one likes to believe this, it must have been a lengthy journey filled with hazard and adventure. Presumably he hired out his sword as he went as did so many other Scots. Finally he reached Northern Italy and apprenticed himself to an armourer. It is possible that he may have waited and made part of the journey in the train of "The Laird of Glenurquay" to whom his younger brother Malcolm was Standard Bearer, on their way to fight the Moors in Aragon. Tradition has it that he went ahead by himself and this is the more likely, for being young and eager to perfect his craft, he would have found it hard to thole the slow and stately progress of a Crusading army.

Eventually his years of apprenticeship were ended and in due course he made his way back to Scotland. As a master-craftsman it must have been an easier journey. In 1440 he was commissioned by the Lady of Glenurchy to make the iron work and to supervise the rebuilding of Kilchurn Castle, while Sir Duncan Campbell was still in Spain crusading against the Moors. So he built his house and forge at Barr á Chaistealain, the Hill of the Castles, above where Dalmally now stands. The Castles were three Pictish Brochs, one of which can still be traced and is marked on Ordinance maps as the Fort. He achieved a considerable reputation as an armourer and swordsmith and is said to have made swords for the King of Scots.

It is often claimed that we go back much further and that Duncan was the son of an earlier chief. Fifty years or so ago, Mrs. K.E. Grant, writing of her mother Christina Macnab in "Myth, Tradition and Story from Western Argyll" said that her forebears practised their craft for seven centuries. Again, the guidebook to St. Conan's Kirk, Loch Awe, describes the carved stalls in the chancel which "show the full coats-of-arms complete with crests and badges of the chiefs who in the old days held land in the neighbourhood" and included in the list of eight is Macnab of Barachastlain. After the name it adds in parenthesis "a family of smiths who lived above Dalmally for 600 years and helped to build Kilchurn Castle".

On the other hand, a certain John Hay Allan published "Bridal of Caolchairn" (the Gaelic spelling of Kilchurn) in 1822, and in his introductory notes, speaks of a visit to Glenorchy Kirkyard where he saw Duncan's gravestone incised, and then still decipherable, with his initials, a hammer, a pair of pincers and a Highland galley, as indeed were the gravestones of such of his descendants who were buried there. He describes it as "a stone whose device, aided by oral tradition, has perpetuated the memory of him over whom it was laid, Duncan Macnab the Smith who in 1440 assisted in the rebuilding of Castle Caolchairn, and was the ancestor of the Macnabs of Barachastlain. His memory is still remarkable in the glen". The words "oral tradition" are important, for Malcolm, the last of the race of swordsmiths to live on the hill, was still there. He died in 1823 aged ninety.

This agrees with the tradition I had from my father that this Duncan was the founder of our Branch of the Clan. My father was born in 1847 and when a boy in Oban, knew Glenorchy well and many of the old people; and Highland memories are long. However from 1440 to 1823 is lengthy enough, and for nearly four hundred years Duncan's descendants practised the art and craft of armoury, handing it on from generation to generation. They were famed for the quality, temper and ornament of their swords, dirks and sgian dubhs. They worked too in precious metals. Some accounts say they were hereditary armours and jewellers to the Campbells of Breadalbane. They certainly worked for them as indeed they did for all who wanted good craft, but they were prouder still of being hereditary armourers to their own Chiefs and Clan.

There young were unruly at times. In 1621 Patrik McAgowin (Mac-a-Ghobhainn, son of the Smith) was sued by Malcolm McOldonycht (Mac Mhol Domhnaich, son of the servant of the Lord) "for striking him with ane sword and for hurting of his hand, also for spoyleing him of his bow and durk, and taking away XXs. from out of his purse. The Assysis haveing tryit and examinit this blood and wrang, convictit the defender in blood and the persewar in trublance", the unfortunate "persewar" seems to have received scant sympathy! I take it that XXs. means twenty shillings. The Black Book of Taymouth records two more such misdemeanours for which Patrik had to find caution for his good behaviour in "fourtie pundis money".

Eleven years later when he had succeeded his father and had become Patrik Gow (Gobha, the smith) another entry states "Sir Colin Campbell of Glenurqhay, Knight, sets to Patrik Gow — for the shortest liver of the two — the two merklands of Barrachastellan".

Patrik's son styled himself Donald McNuer of Barachastalan, Clachan Dysart. McNuer was possible some variant of Mac Oighre or perhaps McNair (meaning heir), for Patrik his father must have been approaching eighty or more when he died in 1681. Clachan Dysart was the old name for where Dalmally now stands. The name means the place of the High God, a small knowe in the strath, and was once a place of Druid worship. Later it became a Christian sanctuary, and later still, the circle of stones was displaced by a heather-thatched chapel and the "Stone of Power" by a sculptured cross. At the end of the eighteenth century the present Glenorchy Church was built there, with all the old gravestones duly preserved in the kirkyard.

Donald, the son of the Patrik mentioned above, died in 1690, leaving three sons — Patrick, John and Calum, and it was this Patrick's son, another Donald, on whose death the prophecy of the tree came true. There was a vast elm by the smithy at the foot of the hill and it had been prophesied long before that when this tree fell, then would the last of the sword-smiths die, and his sons and their sons would scatter, some even to the ends of the earth. Donald grew old. One night there arose a mighty storm. The gale came sweeping down the glen while up on Barachastlain at the height of the storm the old man lay dying. In the morning the tree lay before the smithy and the sons mourned their father.

I cannot trace the date of Donald's death but it was after the Forty-five and by then with the ban on wearing of swords and of the kilt, the day of the Highland swordsmith was over. Before the '45, in fact from the Fifteenth century when they made headpieces, chainmail, swords, spears and arrowheads, there were sons, brothers, nephews and cousins all working there, some down at the foundry and others on the farm on Barachastlain. Now all was changed. Some had gone to fight for Prince Charles with a body of Breadalbain men under Campbell of Glenlyon, for there were Campbells on both sides, as there were Macnabs. Others settled elsewhere or went soldiering.

Donald had four sons, Patrick Dow (dhu the dark haired one) Donald, Alexander (my great-great-grandfather) and Malcolm. As for the prophecy about scattering to the ends of the earth, Patrick Dow's daughter married a Duncan Ferguson. They went to North Carolina. Their great grandson, General Willard Ferguson of the U.S. Army died in 1937. Donald's son, Duncan, served at Waterloo, and was made Deputy Commissary General on going to Canada in 1832 in connection with the building of the Rideau Canal. His grandson Colonel Alexander James Macnab, Retd. U.S. Army, died in 1956. He was "de jure" Representer and Chieftain of the House of Barachastlain, although he never matriculated the Arms.

Although Alexander went no further than Oban, his grandson, my grandfather, was shipwrecked and drowned on his way to the Far East in 1869. Another grandson, my great-uncle John, was Chairman of the Oriental Bank, while my father spent a great part of his life with the Hong Kong & Shanghai Bank in China and the Philippines, where I, myself, was born. Incidentally, my great-uncle Peter built most of Oban on the coming of the railway.

Of the youngest of the four brothers, Malcolm, I know little, except that he wrote Gaelic verse and was a friend of Duncan Ban McIntyre. One day Duncan Ban brought him the fore leg of a kid and asked him to make a sgian or dirk with this as its handle. He returned next day to find it ready for him. Extolling its beauty and craftsmanship, Duncan Ban asked what was the fee. Malcolm said that if he would put all that praise into an extemporary verse in Gaelic that would be the fee. I have a copy of this verse but have not sufficient Gaelic to assess its merit.

The other Duncan of our Branch, who fought at Waterloo as ensign in the 52nd Foot, was, I believe, Malcolm's grandson but I have no written evidence of this. However, he is buried with his forebears in Glenorchy. He left a daughter called Christina, who may possibly have been the mother of the Mrs. K.W. Grant mentioned earlier, but there have been many Christinas in the Barachastlain family.

It was either Malcolm or his brother, Donald, of whom Pennant in his "Tour of the North" in 1769 made his somewhat snobbish remark "In Glenurchie dwells McNab a smith whose family have lived in that humble station since the year 1440 being always of the same profession". As a Sassennach, however, he was not to know that in the Highlands a swordsmith was a man of standing in his clan, and that usually the occupation was hereditary. In 1792 Robert Heron in his "Observations" tells of being shown by Donald and Malcolm a coat of mail and two headpieces made by their forefathers. These may have been taken away by Patrick Dow's son Alexander (not to be confused with his uncle of the same name) who lived in Barran. As the Head of the family he was justified in doing so. He, too, is buried in Glenorchy with the Macnab Arms carved on his tombstone. It is said that at one time he possessed the M/s of Macpherson's Ossian.

This Alexander left a son, John, who left the forge and smithy to a McNichol one of whose descendants told me once that when he was a boy he used to see in the smithy an old broadsword hanging on the wall and left there by the Macnabs. This was a Dr R.R. McNichol who died in Edinburgh a few years ago, when he was a very old man. John's family died out, except for a Peter, the illegitimate son of one of his daughters. Peter took the name of McNab, though his father was a McGregor. He had a son, the Rev. John McNab, Minister of Skegness, who died in 1939.

Years ago I used to have a cutting from the "Oban Times" reproducing a drawing of the interior of the house by a geologist, St. Fond, who went there to see the chain mail and other relics. But now the house has gone, for its stones were used for the cottages of the Irish navvies who built the railway. These too are ruins with most of their stones taken. The descendants of Duncan are scattered, the railway runs over the land they farmed, and cattle graze among the ruins on the hill. The prophecy of the tree has been fulfilled.

NOTES TO "THE HOUSE OF MACNAB OF BARACHASTLAIN"

1.   Bridal of Caolchairn, a rather romantic and Victorian poem based, as its author admits, on a very slight tradition. Malcolm, brother of Duncan, went as I have said to Aragon and "Full proud Glen Urcha's banner bore, and followed in his Baron's train" but when "weary years were gone" he returned and told of Campbell falling in battle. It is said that the Lady of Glenurquay consoled herself with Malcolm and they were duly wed. Meanwhile, "Glen Urcha" had recovered from his wounds, but had a familiar spirit who told him what had happened and summoned up for him "a blast of wind". This landed him safely on his castle on the Bridal night. Sword in hand and disguised as a monk, he burst in and slew Malcolm in the bridal bed. The black-cowled monk was seen leaping from a window on the keep and, thereafter, spent his days in penance at Ardchatten Priory. Presumably the lady never smiled again!

Mr. John Hay Allan's imagination must have run away with him, for no Campbell, and for that matter no Highlander, would have suffered such remorse over the killing of someone who wronged him.

2.   *Waterloo.* Four Macnabs were officers at Waterloo. In addition to the two Duncans of the Barachastlain family, there was Captain Alexander Macnab of the 30th Foot, who belonged to the Barravorich House. He was aide-de-Camp to Picton and was killed at the same time. Fighting on the other side was the Head of the Newton Macnabs as, it is said, ADC to Napoleon. He was taken prisoner and there is a nice story that the English regiment who captured him wanted to shoot him as a traitor. Duncan, then a captain in the Commissariat (what later became the A.S.C.) stormed into their mess full of indignation. They said 'But he was fighting against the English. "Damnit" said Duncan "We've always fought against the English since the days of Wallace". Not quite a true statement but it worked. One likes to think this story is true.

3.   Alexander (1747 to 1814) the son of Patrick Down, had a natural son, Duncan, 1780. Kirk Sessions Records state "Received this day a guinea from Alexr. McNab for his deliquency". His uncle Alexander was one of the Elders who fined him. The money went to the Poor Fund. The records show him in trouble again in 1801. This time a natural daughter Ann. His granddaughter Christina, daughter of his lawful son John, and mother of Peter, got into trouble too, for in the Kirk Session Records of 1846 there is this entry "Compeared Christina McNab, Barachastalan, by citation, who being examined and interrogated, declares that she gave birth to an illegitimate male child, twenty days before Lammas last. Declares that James McGregor, Manager of the Farm of Glengyle in the Parish of Callendar in the County of Perth, is the father of the said illegitimate child". Poor girl. They seem to have been rather tougher on her than on her grandfather! She died not long after and child, Peter, was brought up by an unmarried sister Catherine.

4.   The Gaelic genealogy of the Macnab Chiefs starts with —
Ferchar Og or Abraruach, the first Abbot of Glenorchy (the Red Abbot).

His father was King Fercha Fada died 697 Brother of St. Fillian.

The names of *his* forebears were:—

King Fergus d. 501. 1st Dalriadic King in Scotland, son of Erc. Loarm, his brother. Ethach (Echaidh). King Beadan. Colman. Sneachton. Fergus. Feradach (father of St. Fillan). King Fercha Fada (died 697)

5.   In the census return for 1792 there were at Barachastlain — Males 9: Females 16. So it must have been a sizeable building or buildings.

COPY OF PARTS OF A LETTER WRITTEN BY ARCHIBALD MACNAB OF MACNAB AT HAMILTON, ONTARIO, IN 1847 TO SIR ALLAN MACNAB

A TRUE RECORD
of

The different Houses & Families of The Clan McNab as they descent from the Original Stock and By whom now represented (in the year 1847).

Houses	Represented by	Remarks
Achasan	Miss McNab presently in Hamilton, *Canada* And the Heirs of the late Colonel Robert McNab 91st Highlanders sometime Governor of The Cape of Good Hope — presently residing in By-town (?) (now Ottawa).	This House is the first Cadet upon Record off this Ancient Family. They came off in the Eleventh Century. This Family suffered much along with their Chief in the contests between Baliol and Bruce (vide) "Blind Harry". After "The Bruce" ascended The Throne the forefeiture of the immense Estates of the Chief followed from "Cross McDuff" about three miles from Perth, to "The Siein a' Chatha" in the Braes of Dalquhidder (more than 70 miles of country) was all forfeited upon that occasion. The Irish and Islay McNabs, then banished, are of this Family, also the Newcastle or English McNabs, of whom the celebrated Doctor McNab Physician to the unfortunate Louis the 16th, was a Member. There are many collateral branches of this House which I cannot follow.
Inishewan	Colin McNab Esqr. of Deignish, Scotland and In Nova Scotia by the Heirs of James McNab	This House came off in the 12th Century. Twas the Head of this Family that led the Clan in 45, along with the Duke of Perth's Highlanders, commanded by the Duke. N.B. The Branch of Nova Sococia, obtained the Grant of their Property (The McNab Island) from the Noble The Marquis of Cornwallis for their High character and Respectability while serving under him.
Barravorich	The Heirs of the late Capt Alexr. McNab, 30th Regt of Foot who fell at Waterloo and (?) Mrs. Col. Philpots The McNabs of Belleville, Niagra and Eqquissing, One of this Family.	The whole of this House Emigrated to Canada about sixty years ago.
Barachastlain	Comsy. General Duncan McNab in Candad.	This Family more Anciently The Armourers & Standardbearers of The Chief.

11

Houses	Represented by	Remarks
Arthurstone	The Honble. James McNab Chief Justice of Calcutta, and Lady Dick, relict of the late General Sir Robt. Dick, K.C.B. who fell in India.	This is a very wealthy and distinguished Family. N.B. It was One of this Family who lately acted for the Chief in Edinr.
Newton	The Heirs of the late Sir (?) Edward (?) McNab, Chevalier de St. Louis, Cote de Loire, France and John McNab of Newton, writer to the Signet, Robert McNab of Portend.	This is a very wealthy Family and now of high standing with an estate on the Loire.
Edinample	John McNab, Esqr. Township of Horton, Canada.	This was a distinguished and powerful Branch, but their *"Geann Teigh"* lay close beside his Chiefs and most of his clan upon the Battle Field of Worcester in Support of the Royal Cause of Charles the First and when *Montrose* again unfurled "The Royal Standard" in the Royal cause the Young Rooftree still stood firm by (his yet Younger Chief) under that Banner (and when he fell) he was appointed by Montrose (vide "Montrose Memoirs") to the defence of the Castle of Kincardine, which he and his followers defended with such devoted bravery, that upon the execution of the Gallant Montrose He and all His House were harried and dispersed by Cromwell and all that was restored of the vast Estates of The Chief was the Lady Chieftainnesses Jointure Lands (vide General Monok's order") as still in the Archieves of the last of the Chiefs.
Dundurn	The Heirs of the late Captain Robt. McNab of Dundurn, now by Sir Allan McNab, Knight.	This House is the last Cadet of "That Family" of whom I have above recorded.

N.B. Not having the Ancient chronological Tables of the Family at hand, I cannot be particular as to the different dates.

Hamilton
15th March 1847   (Sgd) McNAB

Note 1. There is no doubt that Archilbald Macnab of Macnab intended Sir Allan Macnab of Dundurn to succeed him.

Note 2. It was found in 1953 that the Newton Branch was in fact Senior to the Arthurstone and therefore further from the succession to the Chiefship than the latter.

Iain's family were armourers from the 14th century up to approximately the 18th century. Their main production were pistols, which were always fully engraved. He also owned some of the Macnab pistols, which were exhibited in London on several occasions. Amongst his collection was a very long and heavy sword. It was a murderous looking weapon and obviously not made for sword play, fencing or ceremony. Iain knew the history of the sword including the name of the unfortunate victim who had been run through by it. It would have taken a very powerful man to wield such an instrument. But I was able to understand and enjoy Iain's appreciation of the arts of forging such a blade and the engraving. It would appear that throughout the world of armoury, rank and status are very closely related to the amount and the quality of the engraving it carried.

It was intended that he should enter business as his father thought that there were too many artists in the family. One well known member was the sculptor Macfarlan Shannon, his uncle. So Iain was trained as a chartered accountant and was due to sit his finals in October, 1914, but by then he was already in France serving in the Highland Light Infantry. Later he was commissioned and gazetted to the 93rd Division 2nd Argyll and Sutherland Highlanders. He fought at Ypres and at the battle of Loos. Later he became a Divisional Machine Gun Officer and was blown up by shell fire and severely wounded. He was invalided out of the Army in 1916. When he was brought in from the battle of Loos, he was obviously given up for dead. But Iain true to character described the experience of being blown up as, like loudly ringing bells, with a strong smell of sulphur and a sense of floating upwards, thinking he was on the way to heaven, but observing his sergeant major was also in the air floating upwards he felt perhaps the Almighty had made a mistake. While pondering on this theory he returned to earth.

The next two years were spent in hospital beds, and indeed there were many more operations and spells in hospital beds to come. On the outbreak of the Second World War he joined the A.R.P. and kept his school, the Grosvenor School of Modern Art open and working. This amount of active service would have been enough for some; but he volunteered for services in the Royal Air Force only to be invalided out in 1942 and again in 1945. Under these conditions he had experienced life in the raw and seen people severly tested. Yet he was always reckless with his health. His operations were countless and he would often say that there was nothing left for the surgeons now.

Figure 2 — *Merchiston School. Edinburgh.*

Iain often said that his first ambition was to be a cartoonist and caricature people and have fun with politics and people. He said "I just love people and their ways, actions and reactions". This great love of people was later to be poured into his engraving. He also did not set out with the intention of becoming a painter. His strongest ambition was to become a sculptor. But his war wounds ended that dream. It was however the sculptural approach that dominated his style, throughout his life in his painting, drawing and engraving. The sculptural feeling for form and structure established his aesthetic personality. This personality is stronger, purer and more personalised throughout his engraving production. Finally he exchanged the sword for the burin.

There is a hard core of opinion in the world of critics, dealers and officials of art organisations that a large body of work is necessary to support a name in art. This body of people however never undertake to sell the quantity they seek especially while the artist is still alive. Iain's production, compared with some artists is a medium one, concise and very even in quality. If we subtract the time that he spent fighting for our liberty and the further years spent in hospitals from war wounds, then such a production as his is truly remarkable. On top of this his integrity was such that he has destroyed the work that failed to meet the standards of his mature judgement. And this is his answer to the hard core of opinion. Diamond cut diamond. Iain has said, "I feel sorry for the poor devils who fall into the hands of indifferent art dealers. They are unable to do this cleaning up".

Figure 3 — *Illustration from the Sculptured Garland. 1948*

2 - The burin, ink and paper

The evolution from pictorial craft to art is always a slow and gradual process. Usually it takes at least two or three generations to effect. In some cases the transition is completed in a life span and we have experienced such a phenomenal development in Iain's life time. The process of evolution from craft to art is also a two way movement and one can benefit the other. To keep both alive craft must assimilate art and art must sublimate craft. We can see this process evolving in the Twentieth Century print revolution and in the overall production of Iain's engraving. The craft process in question concerns the introduction and use of two dimensional cut-out black and white shapes. Essentially the aesthetic nature of wood engraving is the unrelieved black world or a medium of no light. When the block is pierced with the sharp pointed steel burin it is as a light switched on and from that point onwards the burin should continue to delineate and define the form through allowing more light to develop. Any white areas should then only arise from a full development of light determined by a maximum expression of the form with an absolute economy of means. In this aesthetic, form development, the arbitrary application of the white cut-out shape becomes a breach in the logical development and expression of the form. This form aesthetic becomes even more significant when we consider that all the drawn forms are three dimensionally conceived. In Iain's work we find the earlier examples clearly dominated by this illustrators convention, which arises from the world of the book design, to its ultimate resolution in his later work, where the print becomes aesthetically pure and autonomous. The two dimensional cut-out shape has a long standing tradition arising from the illustration design characteristics of the book, magazine, newspaper and advertising. The practice arises from at least two factors which are far removed from the aesthetics of form. A book or magazine needs this kind of optical stimulation to catch the eye of the well known flipping reader. In advertising sledge hammer tactics are often used to arrest attention. Secondly the printers and publishers are not partial to printing large areas of black. The ink is inclined to show through and therefore necessitates a more expensive quality of paper to carry large black print areas. Thirdly the illustration tradition was directed towards the marriage and harmonising of these two book reading requirements with the irregular shapes comprising the light grey print areas falling upon the page either recto or verso to that of the illustration. In this sense the arbitrary two dimensional cut-out element is craft based and thereby aesthetically impure, and furthermore bears no real relationship to the three dimensional images that comprise the subject of the work. The pictorial dimensions are confused and the language is unresolved. In many other fields of print these cut-out illustrative devices still persist. It is also only a device when composition is considered. Even if the illustration is an entirely free shape arranged in a type set environment the limiting rectangle becomes the shape of the actual page. A situation arises similar to that of the opera and advertising, where all three productions result from a combination of three separate art forms. The very fact that each art form must of necessity be pruned to produce a hybrid offspring, precludes free aesthetic growth and development of any one form and the distorted growth is always more evident in the pictorial matter.

Iain's feelings for the past were very strongly felt and the engraving tradition for him was something exciting and alive. He would so often stress that in his case engraving arises from and has its roots in the work of the armourer of great antiquity. This antiquity he shared directly with his family and clan tradition and its long history. There were many occasions when I would be discussing with him many of the engraving qualities unique to him and he would disclaim responsibility for it and say "Ah, we are armourers, it is in our blood". It was never "We were armourers". He never trained or practised as an armourer. And he loved armour and the pieces he possessed. On occasion he would express this feeling another way, "The Macnabs were armourers and I am a Macnab". Psychologically his burin became the sword and his line made visible the cut and thrust of life. Although modern warfare is not likely to reintroduce personal armour again, but if the need had arisen, Iain would have been ready to go into production. He did however sincerely believe in this tradition to the point where he was a part of it. Iain also laid much emphasis and deep feeling on the drawings in the caves of Lascaux. These drawings are the earliest engravings which were cut into the rock face. Earth pigments and vegetable dyes were then pressed into the incisions of the rock. Primitive drawings are always highly charged with meaning. Superficial aspects of form, which today we are continually being asked to swallow, seem never to arise in the art of the primitive. He had no paper, pencils, tube paints or spray guns, just a bare rock face. The prospect of being confronted with such a challenge would sort the wheat from the chaff even before an impression was made on the rock.

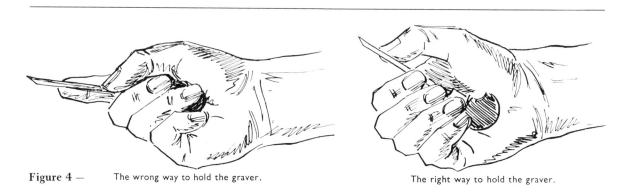

Figure 4 —   The wrong way to hold the graver.   The right way to hold the graver.

Joseph Hecht, a master copper engraver teaching in Stanley W. Hayter's Atelier 17 in Paris is reputed to apply a brutal teaching technique of suggesting to the innocent student during the first lesson to force the burin into the copper plate as deeply as possible. This having been done, the next instruction was to scrape away all trace of the deep incision and retrieve the previously polished surface. Such a heart breaking operation decided whether a second lesson in copper engraving was needed. The main point of the exercise is that students are bound to make mistakes and slips, which have to be scraped out and repolished leaving no trace. Hecht made the student meet this craft requirement at the beginning. It was being cruel to be kind. Regardless of all the arguments on self and imaginative expression that may be brought forward in defence of the student, I feel that Hecht was right. At the other end there is also very little comfort. The public will certainly be mercilessly cool and surgically sharp in judging the quality of engraving. Much more so in fact than is the case with painting and sculpture. This can be seen in the public's critical appreciation of the engraved bank note and the lack of critical appraisal of good or bad painting.

Apart from the very early Chinese work, prints from wood blocks appear to have been first made towards the end of the 14th Century. The oldest known surviving print with a date is a devotional print of 1418, and it is the work of an experienced craftsman. Soon after this, probably between 1420 and 1440, block books were printed and published, in which the text as well as the illustrations were cut on blocks, one for each page. Two of the finest are the Biblia Pauperum and the Ars Moriendi, and both can be seen in the British Museum.

The invention of printing books by means of movable type, that is with separate small blocks for each letter, came about a generation later, and led to the production between 1450 and 1550 of a great number of books magnificently illustrated by wood cuts. The number is so great that it is difficult to name but a few, Holbeins "Dance of death" is the best known. Larger wall prints such as Durer's "Great passion" were also made during this period.

In the 16th Century the increasing interest in light and shade caused artists to explore methods of expressing realistic tone. One result was the chiaroscuro print made by two or more printings from two or more blocks; Hendrik Goltzius (1558-1617) and others produced very fine results. By the beginning of the 17th Century the Italians were using the chiaroscuro print as a means of reproducing the appearance of a tinted drawing, and the end was at hand. The Rococo period had lost interest in the qualities which wood cuts could express so well, and artists were only able to use media which permitted closer rendering of subtle gradations of tone.

In the first half of the 18th Century Papillon in Paris engraved with the burin on the end grain of hard wood. But he was before his time and the world does not appear to have thought as much of his method as he certainly did himself. The place of the wood engravers art as a personal means of expression was obscured during almost the whole of the 19th Century by the use of wood engraving as a reproductive medium, which produced wonderful technical results in the work of Timothy Cole in America, or W.J. Linton, and of Swain and Dalziel in the production of the illustrated books of the "Sixties".

The first English book known to have been illustrated with wood engravings is Howell's "Medulla Historiae Anglicanae", 1712, in which, as the bookseller's preface states, the plates were engraved on wood because copper would be more beautiful but more expensive. These early engravings were made to look like copper engraving.

The armourer from the earliest times engraved on the metal and the starting point gives rise to the quality of expression known as engraving. Like stone sculpture its tough character springs from the resistance of some hard material. The linear aesthetic qualities of the drawings or engravings at Lascaux also spring from the resistance of the hard rock face. Burins are pushed with considerable pressure. The line resulting from it was described to me by the late John Buckland Wright as being sculptural and he also emphasised that there was no other linear medium that is so sculpturally expressive. When discussing these qualities with the late Clifford Webb, he said in reference to the work of Gwenda Morgan, that engraving was possibly the most personally expressive technique an artist can use. Engraving is of course a fundamental discipline. Whilst discussing fundamental disciplines with the American sculptor and typographer Elliott Offner he said "In America at the present time there are a number of significant artists who feel strongly that the time is fast approaching for another look at the fundamental disciplines. We are in real danger of pursuing technical gimmicry and losing out on fundamental expression".

The important link between engraving and sculpture is the resistance set up by the hard materials. In engraving the burin being pushed ahead of the artist's thinking, through the tough materials gives the essential characteristic of the taut, tough and cut character of the line. The tautness and compression of form in carved stone sculpture arising from the resistance by hard materials also establishes an essential difference between the relaxed and free form resulting from sculpture modelled in clay. Similarly in pencil drawing the form is much more free and more relaxed. Drawing with the burin will never produce an engraving and an engraving must never simulate a drawing in any other medium.

An engraving starts at a point just above the pelvis following through to the spine, shoulders, arms, wrists and then to the fingers. It is therefore a very physical experience, demanding strength and unflinching concentration. A steel point travelling through a hard material demands an intellectual precision of thought and the point which travels ahead of the thinking process demands an intellectual agility. The engraver has to keep up with an engraving. In drawing the pencil follows after the decision making. A pencil can always be modified in its tract, a burin on the other hand is always either in track or out, if it is out of track, a mistake has been made which means starting again regardless of the time spent and the cost of the materials. In engraving there are no margins for error. This is a challenge which all engravers must accept. There will never be many top quality engravers in any single generation. Most would be engravers are either killed off by the craft or the personalities are smothered by the strictures of the discipline. When an artist does succeed in riding the engraving wave there will always be a place for him or her in art history.

No artist's medium or technique can compare with the whiteness and blackness of wood engraving. It is the ultimate in black and white expression. The precision and expressive qualities of the engraving line are however common to both wood and copper engraving. Such intense whiteness and blackness which characterises wood engraving are the psycho-physical optical properties, which are at variance with the physical stimulus. The physical qualities of the print stimulate the mind, to produce, psychologically a subjective white and black sensation. Exactly the same phenomenon in experiencing and viewing reproduction on television. In both cases the whites and blacks are seen subjectively, both brighter and darker respectively, regardless of how grey the physical stimulus happens to be.

It has long been accepted that, up to certain levels, the higher the illumination the smaller the detail and objects we can see; the ability of the eye to distinguish fine detail determines the clarity with which objects or lines in a scene are resolved. The actual ability of the eye to detect detail under optimum conditions is remarkable, indeed incredible. Under suitable illumination the eye can detect a black line (against a light background) little more than 0.0007 mm. wide when viewed six inches from the eye. This, of course, also depends on having an optimum eye as well. The whole process of vision is based upon contrast.

Whilst discussing his work George Mackley said, "Before I begin an engraving I must practise myself into a point of emotional, intellectual and optical balance where I am able to cut a minimum of twenty white lines to the inch, which means also that there are at least twenty clearly defined black lines in between and this is with the single burin and not with the aid of a multiple tool." Wladimir Favorsky, the recently late and great Russian wood engraver even exceeded this figure during his peak period between his "portrait of Dostoyevsky", 1929. and "Portrait of the actress Babanova in the role of a boy in Faiko's play, Chelovek is Portfellm", 1933. These two works show greys of from forty to over fifty white and black lines to the inch. Blair Hughes Stanton and Agnes Miller Parker also achieved these effects, which are the prize of superb craftsmanship, sublimated to art. An art so subtle that it is so often unseen and unsung. Iain achieves this optical effect of the shimmering silvery greys in many prints especially in "Southern Landscape" 1933 *Fig.28* and in his final engraving "Ronda Bridge" 1961. *Fig. 34.*

Our eyes must adapt to the available white and black. The amount of light from both gives the objective physical information received through the optical system, which in turn instructs the brain, which then interprets these signals in its own way. Black and white adaption factors of the eye and the adjustment to the physical stimulus is a function of the rod nerve receptors in the peripheral vision area of the eye. The rods are more sensitive to light than the colour cone nerve receptors found at the back and centre of the retinae. Adaption to the available hues and chromatic intensities also takes place in colour vision. The largest areas of colour or black and white then determine the vision field dominance. When looking at a wood engraving after giving our eyes a few seconds to adjust, our field dominance in most cases is black. We are then black adapted. The psychological black is produced as in conditions of very low light. It is virtually near total absorption and the physical optical system just fails to register or respond to such near threshold limits. A state of no light at all can only be experienced in a deep mine, a perfect physics laboratory or underground cave. The physicists ideal black demonstration is a cave in miniature. Demonstrations are usually made with a tin in which a very small hole has been made. A light beam entering the hole is completely trapped and absorbed, which gives the physical absolute black. As soon as the burin enters the block light is being produced in the black field of the print. As in the case of the engraver working on a block, which has previously been given a coating of black ink, so with the print observer, both are dark adapted and in the highest optical state to see the very finest of white lines. Even if the printed paper is a light grey or cream, when seen through the engraved image, either will appear white in the lines. To see black lines on a white surface we need to be white adapted from a white field background. Black lines on a white surface constitutes the public's main conception of drawing and the public are also more practised in reading black on white drawing. This gives rise to a hard core of tradition which resists the introduction of the white line technique. In March 1927 when the engraving revival was gathering momentum a writer in the Manchester Guardian commenting on a Society of Wood Engravers exhibition held in Manchester said "One notices in the show a leaning towards the school of opinion that considers white line on a black ground to be the preferable practice in wood engraving. This opinion certainly has technical reasons to support it and was generally followed by French artists, but a glance round the room makes one feel that black lines on white give a much greater pleasure to the eye. Prints done in this way suggest life and space, whereas many of the opposite type look like interesting coal cellars".

It is this fundamental optical phenomenon upon which the engraving revolution and revival is technically based. Nineteenth Century engraving in art and industry had become essentially a black line process on a white ground, which was virtually an imitation of the drawing process, using instruments other than a block and burin.

An important aspect of all the colour and surfaces that we view in normal life is texture and texture is an essential quality of the black engraved print. The ink used for engraving is strictly speaking not an ink at all, but a paint pigment with an oil vehicle, based upon a generous proportion of boiled or stand oil. Boiled oil is linseed oil, heat treated to evaporate water and to advance the drying process of the oil. Stand oil is quite thick and high is viscosity and has received a longer heat treatment than boiled oil. A high viscosity in oil naturally gives a high gloss finish to paints and oil bound inks. In wood engraving print the high gloss ink finish does not appear when dry. The oil is absorbed in depth, throughout the paper. Ink pigments for engraving are rather large colourant particles which are not soluble in water. These particles are suspended in the oil vehicle but do not colour the oil. The viscosity of the ink and the colourant particle density of the ink are critical for top quality print. If too much oil is present the ink and oil will run across the white lines and foul them, on the other hand if the ink is too stiff the black surfaces will not be completely covered and the black areas of the print will be spotted and imperfect, also if too much ink, even of the correct viscosity is used there will be a surplus to be displaced during printing which will make the edges of the lines ragged and indistinct. This last quality is always referred to as being over inked. Very fine lines which should be visible in the print are also lost through this defective printing quality. The texture of the paper and ink is very fine and the black ink surface is diffusing the reflected and specular light, like velvet. An even diffuseness of this kind is determined by the specular light reflection being evenly distributed by the regular closeness of the paper fibres and the even surface and depth distribution of the ink particles. The diffuseness of the light scattered on the surface and in depth makes the black appear darker than it really is. There is also a very small quantity of blue pigmentation in the black which by illusion helps to increase the sense of blackness.

The aim in artist printing is a perfect ink consistency regulated to the degree of fineness of the engraving and a paper with a texture as sensitive as silk, to enable the minutest detail on the block to be sharply recorded. For the best artist prints hand made Japanese papers are used. These papers are pure natural fibres with no chalk or loading matter, such as is used in machine made commercial papers. Also on machine made papers the ink would dry with an undesirable high gloss surface because of the chalk or loading matter used in their manufacture. This high gloss finish can be seen very clearly in reproductions on magazine art (so called) papers. The distribution of the fibres would be sparse throughout the depth of the paper and the light below the surface would not be satisfactorily refracted and reflected.

Natural materials used for the long fibres in hand made Japanese papers makes the sheet extremely tough for printing. For hand burnished prints toughness is essential. Even if the artist does not print the whole edition, he will in nearly every case burnish the trial proofs. Most of Iain's editions were run off by his printer after he had produced the perfect trial proof for the printer to work to. The silk like texture is consistent throughout the depth of the Japanese papers and through the highly absorbent quality in depth, the ink is drawn throughout the thickness of the paper and the printed image naturally appears on the reverse side of the paper. In commercial printing this quality is an undesirable characteristic and not wanted. Chalk, china clay and other loadings are added to prevent a reverse image appearing on the back, in fact in many commercial products there is very little paper as such. Some are so heavily loaded that they will put fires out. The chalk particles are also there to put the light beam out by total reflection before it reaches through the back.

The Japanese have an intrinsic regard for paper that has virtually no parallel in the Western world. They were quick to realise the potential of the Chinese invention and considered it worthy for the offering to the Gods and the Shinto priests. Most of the papers are produced by Japanese families and the secrets are handed on from one generation to the next, until the family dies out. When this happens the paper and the secret is lost, never to be repeated. The production of such fine hand made papers is a laborious process. Some of the papers of very rare quality are works of very imaginative design and craftsmanship in their own right. Often two, three or more papers will be laminated into a single sheet. In Europe, especially during the two wars Japanese hand made papers were imitated. These imitations always had a hard insensitive surface and were not worth picking up.

There are thousands of years of tradition underlying the production of paper. The demands arise from a society completely different from that of the occidental society. There is little doubt that this lovely material has come to us from the Orient where there is approximately a two thousand year history of hand made paper making. Paper as we regard it today was probably the invention of the Chinese during the Eastern Han Dynasty (A.D. 25-200).

Ts'ui Lin was the first to describe paper in China in A.D. 105. Europe however had to wait until the Twelfth century for paper to be first established by the Moors in Spain. In Europe the utilitarian aspects have tended to dominate the development. Paper in Europe has never assumed quite the same degree of symbolic meaning as is the case in the Orient, neither have objects made of paper been used in the same ceremonial way as in the Far East. In Japan the sensitivity to paper is highly developed both as an art and social language. The design of the paper arises from the fibres and the mutations of their mixtures. In length the various fibres will range from fractions of an inch up to even six inches in length. With such a variation in the lengths of the natural fibres a very wide range of thickness and texture is available. It is the length of range and thickness variation and closeness of distribution by paper area, which gives a range of textures, which is never obtainable in European papers. There are some Japanese hand made papers with textures too rough for the purpose of drawing, and printing and too stiff and crease resistant for even the purposes of folding. In character some are quite mild and no doubt are used for the furnishing of their homes. Very sensitive hand made papers are used for wrapping gifts and the quality of the paper is chosen with a view to pleasing not so much the person who acquired it but the recipient of the gift. The range available also has male and female design characteristics. There is no doubt that the now extensive range which is available arises from the highly developed Japanese custom of giving gifts to please other people. In Europe we use cheap commercial paper and cover it with a printed design. Some very sophisticated shops in London sell very expensive gift wrapping papers with designs commissioned from the very famous artists of the Ecole de Paris, but even these are printed on cheap commercial papers. In Japan this would be too insensitive for the social purpose of gift wrapping.

The Japanese and Chinese developed an art of paper folding called origami, which is an art that apparently shares equal rank with the more familiar arts of painting and sculpture in those countries. It is an art completely linked with the stylized traditions of the Japanese. Folded paper has a role to play in the all important ceremonial etiquette of Japanese social life. An origami form is used to complete the paper decorations attached to the gifts. The forms will be created by and are unique to the person giving the present and pleasant for the recipient. A complete and individual statement. In Europe paper folding is ranked as a craft and not given the status of an art. No doubt this is due to our inability to be creative enough in this particular field to raise the craft to the level of art.

Many versions of hand made Japanese papers are made from the fibres of the mulberry tree and the rice plant. Such a paper is the Hosho paper made from the bark of Kozo (paper mulberry) and is highly prized by the Japanese print artist. This paper has been used for making prints from the time when prints began to be developed. Another famous paper is made largely from the bark of gampi (Wilestraemia) with an addition of wood pulp or manilla fibre. This one is known as Torinoko. In colour it is a rich cream and in texture silklike, and is tough, even and firm. A very wide variety of papers are made from the rice plant. The range of natural fibres is virtually limitless. It is these paper qualities that enable the Japanese print artists to practise their mastery at splitting the values of black to surgical limits and precision. They are also masters in the manipulating of the "just observable differences" in the hue range and selection at the dark tips of the visible spectrum. The lengths to which some Japanese artists are prepared to go, by contrast, just demonstrate another area of occidental insensitivity.

The famous Japanese artist Maki Haku, born in 1924 and now living in Tokyo had this to say regarding the printing of his impression entitled "Ushi" (Ox), which was a black and white print using only shape and wood textures. "Four blocks (cherry, lauan and sen) of both solid board and plywood were used. One block was printed in gaufrage to define the outer limits of the print with its embossed line, and the other parts in sumi ink and black Japanese-style pigment on natural-colour kozo paper. One impression for the gaufrage block and two impressions each for the black blocks". The elderly master of print Hiratsuka Uni'chi, born 1895 and resident in Tokyo and an expert on hand made Oriental papers goes much further in printing sensitivity. When describing the technique of his print entitled "Byodo-in Chihan" (Byodo-in Lakeside) he has this to say. "The print image is carved on a single board of honoki (magnolia obovata.T) with a single flat chisel, seven millimeters wide, called an aisuki. It is printed on hodomuro paper from the Fukui Prefecture, used raw without the usual dosa sizing in order to allow the sumi ink (Ryu'un from a Kyoto maker specialising in traditional ink) to sink into the paper to give depth to the print. Self-printed with many impressions of different parts (up to fifteen or sixteen for the lake area) to achieve the degree of blackness desired. The printing of each copy required about thirty minutes, with more than sixty unsatisfactory cast-offs". These two print artists give an excellent practical demonstration of splitting black values through using the penetration of light below the surface of the paper which was described previously in a scientific manner. With craft of this order, the attending complexities of the registration of each printing just does not bear thinking about.

If we take a look at the present hand made paper situation in this country, we then find that we have already lost a number of famous hand made papers which have been on the market for several generations. The demand and market is still there. These valuable papers have been lost for no other reason than big brother taking over little brother and throwing out anything which happens to be a nuisance to big brother. The scrapping of the Whatman and David Cox and other papers is always given as a difficulty of finding enough men to work on hand made paper when they can earn more money making commercial paper on long mass produced runs. There is no English hand made paper with a colour range for printing available. The manufacturers are loathe to dirty their equipment with colour. But a sizeable market exists for such a range. Perhaps the day is approaching when the artist will design and make his own paper. Who knows this may not be a bad thing.

Iain's technical masterpiece in this category is his print *Fig. 28* "Southern Landscape", 1933. It is a remarkable technical achievement and a very fine example of the shimmering silvery greys peculiar to wood engraving only. The silvery greys arise from the exacting control of the way and the amount of light which is allowed to penetrate the black and the white lines which must be narrow enough not to appear optically white. These qualities are rare and appear to be restricted to the best English and Russian wood engraving. Although the quality of reproduction of this book is good, there is however no hope of reproducing a high fidelity of these silver greys by mechanical means.

Iain was also very sensitive to the texture of materials. In "Southern Landscape" 1933 he set out to create not only the form of the curtain on the right but the texture of the fabric as well in pure free white line. When discussing this print with him he emphasised that no multiple tool of any kind was used, each line is its proper length and each one running parallel to the other with no fluffing or slipping and the curtain took him three weeks to engrave. I asked him why he went to such lengths and he replied. "I had to put the engraver to the test, just to see if he was the engraver that he thought he was". He was always very proud of this print. Like the two Japanese artists all of them with no thought of appreciation or hope of financial reward set out with aims to a limit and then worked to manifest the virtually impossible for all but a few. The creation of a masterpiece is its own reward and this sensation can never be taken away. With the passage of time the interest in masterpieces may fluctuate, but they are always there, setting the aims and giving encouragement to others and pleasure to many. The full appreciation of this print does however extend into the sensitive printing and inking and the silky iridescent surface of the hand made paper.

An end grained box wood block in itself is a beautiful thing. The craft involved in their making is of a high and exacting order and many an engraver has kept a block which is just so fine that they have hesitated to cut the surface. End grained blocks are essential for engraving. It enables the burin to cut clean furrows with even pressure, freely through the perpendicular and evenly spaced fibres. As the fibres are perpendicular then there is no opening or closing of the furrow once the burin has made its cut. The action of the cutting is precise. This is not the case with the wood cut which is done with a knife on a long grained timber plank. Cutting with the long grain is clean and precise, but cutting across the grain is much less precise. The need to cut across the long grain fibres and along the fibres does give the broader, freely cut character which is the essential feature of the wood cut. Although the means of producing these two print mediums is closely related but different, a wood cut cannot be in any way similar to a wood engraving print.

The development of an end grain boxwood block starts with the selection of the timber. This selection must give an evenness of grain quality all over the surface. Colour changes in the timber will indicate a change of growth and therefore hardness. The boxwood is firstly sawn into one inch thick pieces across the trunk of the tree, then the pieces must be stacked to dry and season for a long time in such a manner that the air can circulate freely through the stack. This process takes many years to complete. A boxwood tree is never very large. In Mr. T.N. Lawrence's famous workshop at Bleeding Heart Yard, just off Grenville Street, Hatton Garden, London, a meeting place for engravers from all parts of the world, I have seen boxwood rings approximately fourteen inches in diameter, which for boxwood is very large and an average ring would be more like six to eight inches in diameter. The growth rate of the box tree is very slow and this gives a very close gap between the annular rings produced from summer and winter growth. Boxwood like any other timber dries from the outside sapwood to the inner core and in the process of contraction it will develop star shakes along the radial lines moving outwards from the centre. In the made up block naturally these shakes must be cut away because the radial lines move into the centre. The outer rings which are lighter in colour are younger and also have to be cut away as it is sap wood and therefore much softer and it will rot, breakdown or twist much more quickly than the older inner hard wood. Printing blocks are all made up to the type high measurement, which is the height of a shilling. Whatever size an end grain block is, it has to be made up with every joint perfect and tongued and grooved. Each piece has to be carefully selected for colour and grain quality. The final surface must be flat and perfect form all blemishes and with a high polish arising from the fine finish of the timber and nothing else. Even the slightest dent or scratch on the surface will print white. The finished block may appear quite simple, just a flat piece of timber type high, but it involves an extremely high development of craft in the making of them. Kenneth Lindley, a younger generation engraver, in his book, "The Woodblock Engravers" says, "The actual process of blockmaking appears from verbal description to be very simple, but it is this very simplicity which proves the remarkable skill of the blockmaker. In fact Mr. Lawrence reckons to train an apprentice for at least five years before he is capable of producing blocks of the standard required for engraving. It is hardly surprising that craftsmen blockmakers are rare indeed and difficult to replace". He then continues, "The sources of boxwood for blockmaking have varied considerably over the years. Most of the wood used in the last century came from the Caucasian mountain region. Some of the logs were of exceptionally large diameter and must have come from very ancient trees. The Russians finally ceased to export the wood from this area in 1935, when a substitute known as East London boxwood was found (named from the port which serves the district in which it is grown). This wood was of excellent quality, with some trees of large diameter, but the supply dried up after twenty-five years because of the danger of soil erosion caused by excessive felling.

The wood used today comes mostly from Venezuela and is known as West Indian box. It is softer than some of the others but the trees are large. A little English box is used and a supply of very hard wood from Persia is just coming into use".

Because of its hardness and density boxwood has a very high permanency rating and we find the boxwood sculpture of the 16th Century German school still in a perfect state of preservation.

In wood engraving there are many built in restrictions, both from the point of view of art and the craft, and the question is often raised and phrased as "why always in black and white and why not in colour". The field of colour in wood engraving has been extensively researched by many leading engravers particularly over the last forty years or so. A starting point on the development of form in colour in a print medium must be that there is no point in or gain in any medium at all unless the effects are entirely unreproduceable by any other means. Secondly on the aesthetic plane whatever the medium, the colour must be satisfactorily married to drawing, form and space concepts. Thirdly, given the first and second requirements it must then by means of colour extend the expressive range of the medium. Colour in all the print mediums is developed on the principle of overlapping layers of hues articulated through the trichromatic system. For infinity of spatial development as in etching, lithography and the wood cut, detailed control of ink distribution, the two qualities of thickness giving both transparent and opaque effects are essential properties required for each and every layering of the ink on the plain surface of the block. Given these two qualities a third is required in the form of a controlled textural break up of the ink film, such as in lithography there is the grain of the Bravarian limestone. In the wood cut there is the grain of the timber plank and in etching there is the biting of the acid. The last element finally decides the build up of three dimensional images and the space corollary. Failing any of these aspects then colour can only be used and developed in a two dimensional world of shapes only. Colour is essentially spatial. The breaking up of shapes into small overlapping areas may create the illusion of three dimensional solids, but it still refuses to add up in terms of space. Therefore in the aesthetics of form illusionistic techniques are untenable and throw us back into the Victorian era of the formless sentimental illustrator.

The inherent colour limitation in wood engraving is based upon the perfectly flat surface of the end grain boxwood block and the inevitable even and regular distribution of the ink film, which makes wood engraving essentially a line block medium. Any line block medium must print colour as a flat unbroken shape or area.

Iain experimented in colour and his print entitled "Canterbury Pilgrims", 1938, not illustrated is in colour and designed as a pair of blocks, which give the colour separations. In this work, commissioned by the Samson Press, which was reproduced in Thomas Balston's book entitled "English Wood Engraving 1900-1950", the artist accepts all the limitations previously defined and uses colour as a pure decoration, or embellishment, flat and two dimensional in treatment. As an engraving it is even doubtful if it gains anything at all from the introduction of colour. Seeing it as an illustration is another matter. Even using colour in the inherent flat line block treatment there are serious limitations, the full range of value, or light reflection cannot be used. All the very light hues destroy the total form and also defeat the optical values of the engraving itself. Also there are very restricted limitations on the use of chroma. Hues of high chromatic intensity will not marry satisfactorily with black. They become optically untenable and aesthetically negative. These inherent restrictions then limit the successful but narrow range of hues to the tertiary hues, low in chromatic intensity and relatively low in value or light reflection. There is however a useful though restricted range of colour from the centre to the dark pole of the colour solid that can be usefully exploited where the art is purely abstract in language. The way through to space expression must however be developed by and through the line block two dimensional shape. It is however this restriction that will be responsible for the few significant works in colour.

A hall mark of a good engraver can also be seen in the way the engraved blocks are completed, especially when large areas of white have to be carved away. After the linear work has been completed, carving begins in the removal of the surplus white areas by the lowering of these areas. This carving away of the white areas should be a continuation of the engraving process and performed with very sharp tools. All the cut away parts are then still formally related to the design. There is no print reason whatsoever for this continuation into carving. It is simply a matter of pride, craft and a respect for lovely materials. The blocks are beautiful objects in their own right. Every cut is sharp, clean and crystal clear and each cut is related one to the other. Sharp tools are the first line of defence against the fatal split.

In a recent letter to me George Mackley had this to say on wood engraving. "I find satisfaction in seeing a work of imagination in which the content has been embodied in a structure of design supplied by the engravers intellect. As you would guess without my telling you, I like to see all the engraver's resources of craftsmanship used in support of his creative imagination. I never could see why, because a work is imaginative in character, it should have to appear as if the design on the block had been gnawed out by mice. The current cult of incompetence does not win my respect. Wood engraving must look like wood engraving." George Mackley and Iain were great friends and professional companions. It was Iain who introduced me to him and his work. Iain said of George's engravings, "Just look at them, they are always very small and hard to find." It is also a memorable experience to see George Mackley's face when he was talking about mice. I remember John Buckland Wright saying, "A masterpiece is often the most easily passed by in exhibitions".

3 - The art of engraving

The main focus of our interest in engraving begins with the engraver ghosts of Fleet Street. Today the ghost is disreputable though respected, and revered for a fabulous skill, which is now aesthetically valueless. During the Nineteenth century, engraver and artist joined forces to give the press visual reproduction of the days events. Science, art and industry came together within their wide ranging fields to produce a new type of artistic expression.

Visual art, unlike architecture, does not lend itself naturally to a division of labour. Although there are historical paintings worked upon by two artists or by a master and student, there is no significant example of this co-operation in drawing. Fleet Street, however, always resourceful and ruthless, found a way in the Nineteenth century of interpreting the work of the artist through the engraver, which did lead to a forced division of labour. Yet until quite late in the century the artist was the only producer of pictorial news for multiplication through the printing presses serving the rapidly increasing numbers of newspapers and magazines. Pictorial news is dependent upon two vital factors, time and clarity of image, and the ultimate of both elements is newsprint run on the rotary press. In those days the unit upon which the artist and printer had to work was a line drawn and printed in black ink.

To make the printing of pictorial news possible Fleet Street had to adopt the relief system and make line blocks from wood or metal upon which the drawn image was a flat surface to take the ink, and the depression between the raised surface lines were carved or engraved to ensure clean white paper between the drawn lines. Such a displacement of wood or metal is an exaggeration of the art of engraving. The simplest form of engraving is a scratch below the surface of some hard material. When the scratch is filled with black ink a sheet of paper is laid on to it, and the material and paper are passed through two rollers under pressure; the ink will be pulled from the groove giving a perfect impression of a black line. Black lines below the surface of the vehicle are referred to as intaglio printing. If the ink is rolled on to the surface and not into the scratch and a print is taken, a perfect impression will result, but the line will be white on a black surface and a relief print will have been made. Newsprint had to be based upon the relief system with the added benefit of less roller pressure being required than for intaglio printing.

Fleet Street's problem in meeting the insatiable demand for pictorial news was the production in large numbers of a type of engraver who would suppress all his individuality and concentrate entirely upon the mechanical skill and commercial development of the technique of engraving only. The nucleus of commercial engravers was built up from gold and silver smiths, jewellers, watch makers and gunsmiths.

Two kinds of engraving were used, steel and end grained boxwood. Steel did not gain general favour as it is very tough and, though fine in quality, cost more to engrave. It was also difficult to repair, or to alter. Furthermore, it did not lend itself to Fleet Street's ultimate desire for the division of labour on the engraved block itself. The higher skill has its limitations and the effort to close the time gap between the event and the publication date was remorseless. End grained boxwood allowed the division of labour to become a reality.

A new industry developed in the manufacture of boxwood blocks, which were type high, an international measurement based upon the shilling. All the world's printing machinery is made to take blocks and formes type high. The shilling happened to be handy for Caxton's measurement and it has never been changed. It is also possible that the change over to the decimal system will not change it now. A boxwood block could be cut into two, four, six or eight pieces and bolted together on the back face. This enabled a publisher or printer to farm out a single drawing as a number of pieces to several engravers. Then a senior or foreman engraver or finisher would bolt the engraved pieces together and finish the work across the joins so that no trace of the breach appeared on the final paper impression of the reproduced drawing. All the drawings were traced on to the surface of the block and then engraved in reverse.

The skill in commercial engraving reached phenomenal heights during the period from the Crystal Palace Exhibition of 1851 to approximately 1880. Form and space were rendered with the sharpest printed image on newsprint. As the form was so clearly stated any amount of detail could be carried with equal precision, without the image appearing fuzzy and laboured. These particularly desirable qualities have rarely been achieved in news and magazine print since. On the time aspect, the great record was achieved and maintained by The Engineer, a weekly publication. About 1870 to 1875, this publication had narrowed the news time gap between the event and publication to ten days.

Such demands and commercial incentives on their craft resources caused individual commercial engravers to develop skills other than those which rightly belong to their medium. For one thing the prima donna artists whose eyes and hands recorded the event or scene, were naturally not willing to have their styles and techniques slaughtered by the engravers. Hence the engravers even turned their skills to facsimile interpretations of the artist's drawings, rendered in pen, and the degree of their success must be admitted. It is ironical that today we can photograph the commercial engravers very small works into architectural dimensions and use them as murals in fashionable restaurants and coffee bars, where many of the present generation are seeing them for the first time. We are even seeing these works in a way and on a huge dimensional scale which was not possible for the creators at the time in which they lived.

The commercial engravers were interpreters, working in a period when the standards of artists draughtsmanship were very high. This attainment was not unusual, as we in Britain can look back on a good history of achievement by artist draughtsman and artist engravers; but it was particularly in the Victorian era that both the draughtsman and commercial engraver developed together. If the artist decided to live by commissions from the Street he had to acquire confidence in expression by the exacting, uncompromising and revealing pen. This forming factor is often overlooked in their critical evaluation. Today many artists would shudder at the thought of a pen, or graver for that matter. Neither instrument allows for error.

Figure 5 — *Pistols.*
Illustration from 'Robert Browning' 1938

Possibly one of the finest draughtsmen of the Street was Charles Keene (1823-1891), famous for his drawings for Punch. Whistler ranked Keene as comparable with Hogarth. There are many who would still support this evaluation. George du Maurier (1834-1896), the author of Trilby, and Phil May (1864-1903) also contributed fine drawings to Punch. (Du Maurier was of French origin and became completely Anglicised). These names can still be seen, carved in the round table in the board room at the offices of Punch. Rossetti, Millais and Holman Hunt of the Pre-Raphaelite Brotherhood (1849-1890) and Leighton, Pinwell, Sandys and many other artists were not slow to turn their skills to the production of illustrations for magazines and newspapers. None of the group, except Sandys, had however, much conception of the sense and limitations of wood engraving and drew as the spirit willed them. All the artists nevertheless expected the commercial engravers to produce a facsimile reproduction of every penstroke and even the exact width of the penstroke, and that an acceptable rendering of their wash drawings would appear, was taken for granted. This is the period where engraving, essentially a white line medium became a black line process, and later form the basis for a strong reaction and engraving revolution in the Twentieth Century. Rossetti's protests at the mutilation of his drawings by engravers were trenchant, but no craftsman, however accomplished would ever have been able to satisfy him. Some of the earlier artists admittedly did suffer a loss of individuality through engraving in the first half of the Nineteenth century.

For instance, Geoffrey Grigson wrote in a catalogue entry of English Romantic Art, 1947, on the work of Thomas Stothard, R.A. (1755-1834), "Too well known for his book illustrations, which become insipid under the engraver's hand, and now too little known for his paintings". This prompts a question. Where are all the original drawings. They may be worth looking at. There may well be other and unrecorded artists smothered beneath the graver's translations.

The commercial engravers were finally defeated by the birth of photography. Though artists and engravers seemed to have entrenched themselves firmly in the basic forms of large scale illustration, it was only a question of time before their manual skills were threatened and finally defeated by the invention of photography. In 1839, Daguerre, a Frenchman, produced the first shadow pictures by light rays and mechanical means. His first photograph, a still life, in composition was influenced by the painting of the period. Indeed the whole of the Victorian development of photography was strongly influenced by the art of the period. In the following fifty years photography developed with increasing momentum into a respectable industry, which not only changed Fleet Street but the whole of the worlds art and illustration. The photograph relieved the artist of his responsibility to the public to supply pictorial news. Alongside this blessing too the artist had to say goodbye to a source of income, and look cheerful. Commercial engravers were in turn confronted with a new form of picture. Photography's processes were eventually even to provide the means for its mechanical reproduction. The shadow picture also provided a reality to another Fleet Street dream. The time gap between the event and publication closed rapidly to reach the present exciting position of "the same day". It is difficult to give an exact date for the introduction of the first half-tone block, mechanically produced by process engraving and the etched screen, but by 1890, half-tone reproductions of photographs began to appear in several magazines. Punch used its first process or half-tone block in 1892.

The commercial engravers' reply to these intruders was a stiffening of the ranks and a death leap forward to even greater skill. Tint tools were brought into use which would cut several fine white lines at one stroke. With these tools the engravers aimed at facsimile reproductions of the dreaded photographs; and to show their skill in handling tone or variations of grey, they even "Interpreted" paintings. But with this frantic and final development commercial engraving entered its short and final phase. The art lost all its identity, and is now popularly regarded as a disreputable ghost.

Within one century the historical process of the rise and decline of the three periods — early, middle and late — began and ended in the same way as the architectural development of the Doric, Ionic and Corinthian Greek, or the Gothic periods of Norman, Decorated and Perpendicular styles. Throughout history western man has moved beyond and thus destroyed all the forms of stylistic expression he has created with such energy and labour, love and care. The early period contains the new seed and the rugged forms, in the second period the seed reaches a peak of development where the earlier forms are refined; and in the final period the growth of the idea declines, skill takes over and ends in either exaggeration of the art or material or in excessive and retrogressive decoration of the form.

In the late Eighteenth century and early Nineteenth century in the north of this country, an engraver was working independently practising the art of engraving. He was completely in opposition to the main stream at the time and was engraving creatively and direct on to the block in the manner of the white line. This engraver was to be rediscovered and given high praise, which would the better have been bestowed on him during his life time. But with all our intelligence and sensitivity of today we are no better at discovering real worth than they were centuries ago. The engraver and illustrator in question was Thomas Bewick (1753-1828) of Newcastle-on-Tyne and he was to play a real part in the engraving revival and revolution which was to take place in the Twentieth century. Now there is a considerable amount of writing published on his life and work. Virtually all our literature on engraving exaggerates his influence and the part played in the development and revival of the art of engraving during this century. In many discussions with Iain, we enjoyed similar views as to the real significance of Bewick to modern engraving. We both agreed that he was grossly overrated as an influence on the art of engraving, but not of the technique. John Buckland Wright held similar views and said, "But Bewick if we compare his work to a few wood engravings made by William Blake for Thornton's ' Virgil ', he falls into his place as a little master." Thomas Carlyle on reading

Bewick's "Memoir" 1862 wrote to his friend John Ruskin and described the artist as: "Not a great man at all; but a very true of his sort, a well completed and a very enviable-living therein communion with the skies and woods and brooks, not here in ditto with the London fogs, the roaring witchmongeries, and railway yellings and howlings." While Ruskin recommended the "Memoir" for all his drawing students, his reply to Carlyle was, "The only qualification of his admiration was that Bewick, untrained, unhelped, but also unharmed, could draw the poor, but not the rich; he could draw a pig, but not a Venus; because, he was not a gentleman, and he regretted a little Bewick's ' love of ugliness which is in the English soul? ' to be found in Hogarth and Cruikshank," Ruskin's conception of a gentleman was not the usual one, and he describes him in his "Modern Painters" as; "A gentleman's first characteristic is that of fineness of structure in the body, which renders it capable of the most delicate sensation; and of structure in the mind which renders it capable of the most delicate sympathies — one may say, simple, ' firmness of nature '. This is, of course, compatible with heroic bodily strength and mental firmness; in fact, heroic strength is not conceivable without such delicacy. Elephantine strength may drive its way through a forest and feel no touch of the boughs; but the white skin of Homer's Atrides would have felt a bent roseleaf, yet subdue its feeling in glow of battle, and behave itself like iron. I do not mean to call an elephant a vulgar animal; but if you think about him carefully, you will find that his non-vulgarity consists in such gentleness as is possible to elephantine nature; not in his insensitive hide, nor in his clumsy foot; but in the way he will lift his foot if a child lies in his way; and in his sensitive trunk, and still more sensitive mind, and capability of pique on points of honour. " Bewick's famous engraving of an elephant is a "tour de force" of form and volume with all the Ruskinean "fineness of nature", but the elephant is naively related to the landscape and the "Elephantine strength may drive its way through a forest and feel no touch of the boughs". Bewick's aesthetic development fell short of achieving Atride's sensitivity to the bent rose-leaf, but his "The Wild Bull at Chillingham" is sensitively related to the landscape.

In 1775 the Society of Arts offered a prize for "the best engraving on wood or type metal capable of being worked off with letter press". This prize was won by Bewick with fine wood engravings based on prints in Croxall's "Fables". Bewick is essentially an illustrator, but a good one. His most well known work being "Fables", "History of Quadrupeds" and "History of British Birds". His most original work is the long series of small head and tail pieces depicting scenes from the country life, which was very dear to him. An illustrator does not experiment with the language of form, as does the artist and thereby add to our experience and appreciation of it. He records and comments on visual life and in Bewick's case the skill and comment is remarkable. Thereby his quality as an entertainer is naturally high. The quality of an illustrators comments are his most important contribution to art as a whole. We must however admit, any illustrator in this country working representationally with cats, dogs, horses, ducks, geese and foxes cannot but help collect an inflated paper reputation.

Ironically today his small boxwood blocks are changing hands in the sale rooms for sums of up to two hundred and fifty pounds each. His popularity now extends to his blown up prints being used for shop window display. Even on this scale his prints hold their vital quality of engraving. Drawings in other media do not hold up so well when blown up very many times their natural size. In 1937 Iain was commissioned by the London North Eastern Railway to do an engraving for a poster advertising Whitby. The actual print, "The Quayside, Whitby Harbour", is 24.1 x 28.8 cm and in the poster it is blown up to the size of 49.6 x 60.2 cm and the poster effect is very powerful. Iain's poster would, as with the commercial engravers stand up well at even double this size. This is a powerful poster technique, which has just not been seen or even exploited in modern publicity. It can convey a very powerful message a very long way. At a distance it has the engraving quality of high readability at a maximum optical distance. From the point of view of newsprint reproduction wood engraving has no parallel.

In 1889 two young artists, Charles Ricketts and Charles Shannon worked in the wood cut and wood engraving and published Longus's "Daphnis and Chloe" and Marlowe and Chapman's "Hero and Leander". The blocks in both cases were cut by the artists. They also published a magazine called, "The Dial" and it ran for five issues. This magazine also contained blocks cut by themselves, Pissarro and Sturge Moore. From 1896-1904 Ricketts and Shannon were running the Vale Press and produced many volumes which contained further examples of these artists creative engraving. 1894-1914 saw the birth of Lucien Pissarro's Eragny Press.

Pissarro's books were more concerned with relating illustration to type rather than on creative engraving. 1897 saw the publication of William Strang's "Prodigal Son" in Singer and Strang's "Etching, Engraving," etc. A unique example of the use of white line and no black outlines.

At the turn of this century new moves were being made which were to develop into a complete print revolution. Pissarro and Noel Rooke were working and conferring together on multi-colour printing from wood blocks. In 1905 Noel Rooke was appointed Teacher of Book Illustration at the Central School of Arts and Crafts. Rooke had spent a lot of time in French art circles in France and Pissarro a Frenchman had been in England several years, and both appeared completely unaware of the development of the modern wood engraving in France, which got well under way during the First World War. It would appear that Rooke began to engrave in wood in 1904. At this time he was in close contact with William Johnston, from whom Rooke had received his training. Eric Gill a fellow student with Rooke also studied with Johnston and they were all becoming interested in developing a graver-designed technique in wood. It was in 1912 that Rooke began at the Central School of Art to train students in the new art of wood engraving. William Johnston who was an imaginative teacher and organiser took the new approach to wood engraving to the Camberwell School of Arts and Crafts. Eleven years after Rooke had started the movement, there were published in 1915 two small books which were the first to contain modern wood engravings. Eric Gill's "The Devils Devices" was published by the Hampshire House Workshops and Gwendolen Raverat's "Spring Morning" was published by Poetry Bookshops.

The contemporary development of wood engraving as we know it today was well under way in France. In France the technique had been rediscovered by Auguste Lepere and Gusman and they founded the Societe de la gravure sur Bois Originale before the First World War. All the evidence points to a simultaneous, but entirely unconnected and influenced development in both countries. In both countries the Ghost engravers had been at work achieving identical ends. They had created the climate for a revival. Later on when the new art really got under way the critics used the French engravers to hammer our native talent. There was nothing new in that critical technique and there are times when it is justified. The justification being only the stimulation of interest.

Edward Johnston was responsible for re-developing the art of calligraphy at a time when it was at its lowest ebb. 1906 saw the publication of his book "Writing and Illuminating and Lettering'" It was at this time that the Central School of Arts and Crafts were to play such an important role in the early stages of the print revolution. Johnston met W.R. Lethaby the Founder and Principle in 1898. It was Lethaby's suggestion that Johnston should teach calligraphy. In 1899 Johnston had a class of seven, which included Noel Rooke and Eric Gill. Both these students were to make a remarkable impact, not only on the art of lettering but also in the revival and creation of a new language of wood engraving. In fact it was this team of talent, which at a future date were to bring these two arts together in the "Kid Glove Book" development. The teaching direction of these arts and crafts spread into Camberwell School of Arts and Crafts with Johnston as Principle. Johnston was also teaching for at least thirty years at the Royal College of Art. His block letter designed for the Underground Railways influenced Eric Gill's later but similar letter which is used as the typeface for Gill Sans.

The next artist to enter the wood engraving field was Gwendolen Raverat who was a student at the Slade School of Fine Art where no interest was shown in the medium and the craft at the time. From these beginnings unknown to the general public the development of wood engraving was spreading among the younger artists. Soon the first articles on the new art began to appear, and these were to be published in the only two issues of the magazine "Change". Nine engravers were mentioned. In January "The Studio" published its first article on the engravings of Gibbings.

In 1920 the Society of Wood Engravers was formed. The first exhibition was held at the Chenil Gallery in Kings Road, Chelsea during November. This exhibition marked the launching of the new wood engraving, wood cut and the later relief print revival. The society was formed by Robert Gibbings. There were ten founder members Edward Gordon Craig, E.M.O'R. Dickey, Robert Gibbings, Eric Gill, Philip Hagreen, Sydney Lee, John Nash, Lucien Pissarro, Gwendolen Raverat and Noel Rooke. A very strong team. The non-members who were exhibiting at the first exhibition were also individuals destined to contribute to the future development, including Desmond Chute, E.F. Dagleish, Miss Dorothy M. Elliot, Rupert Lee, Miss Margaret Pilkington, Ludovic Rodo and Ethelbert White. The first meeting of this newly formed society was held in Philip Hagreens Studio on March 27th 1920, and the first resolution entered in the minutes of that meeting reads "That this Society be called the Bewick Club". The minutes close on the following declaration of policy. "The purpose of the Society is to hold exhibitions devoted solely to wood cutting and engraving by the European method". At a second meeting on April 9th 1920 in Mr. Dickey's studio it was suggested that a new title be chosen for the Society and that an exhibition be held in the Autumn. It was decided at the fourth meeting in Robert Gibbings studio, that the Society in future be called The Society of Wood Engravers. The practice of holding their meetings in a member's studio has continued up to the time of Iain's death. Also the practice of a minimum number of rules and regulations has been maintained up to today.

At the first exhibition prints by Eric Gill, Desmond Chute, E.M.O'R. Dickey, Gwendolen Raverat and John Nash were on sale at ten shillings and sixpence, (unframed price), a majority at one to three guineas, and Gordon Craig was the most expensive at six guineas each. The total sales at this exhibition realised £268.6.0. For an exhibition of small works and all in black and white, these results must have been considered satisfactory. But looking back on this exhibition, most of these prints now, if obtainable will have gained at least one pound a year in market value. The value for some of them would be very much greater in the present day market. It is also worth recording that Campbell Dodgson, Keeper of Prints at the British Museum, writing the foreword for the first catalogue, confidently predicted that the future would confirm his optimistic views, and it did. "All of the group now entering into association naturally followed the traditional European technique whether they cut with a knife on the plank, or engraved with a burin on the end grain of the boxwood block. The print, whether by rubbing or with the press, with printer's ink, using, that is to say, an oil medium in combination either with black or with coloured pigment, and do not employ the methods which other skilful artists have borrowed from the exotic art of Japan. The tools, material, and processes are just what they have been for centuries; it is only the artists who are different. They may study with advantage the masterpieces of the past, for wood engraving in Europe has a glorious record, but we shall not, if we are wise, exact from them imitation. Let them be themselves, frankly of their own time, and develop a modern style. If it is good it will make its impression, tomorrow if not today. If it is not good, there's an end to it. In art everything is worth doing; the great requisite is that it must be well done. The woodcuts must be good, and now, tomorrow if not today, they will be bought and prized. The collecting public mostly consists of persons who frame prints and hang them on their walls; the more advanced type, already far gone on the road to ruin or financial greatness, who keep them in boxes, is rarer. It is for the modern engraver to convince the public that a wood cut looks as well on a wall as an etching, if not better. He should not find it difficult. The present exhibition, I should hope, will not close without amply proving the case. The wood cut has an illustrious past, an exciting, enquiring present, and, let us hope, a brilliant and prosperous future". This future was to witness the redevelopment of all the range of print media.

The press reaction to the first exhibition was remarkable. Reviews were published in no fewer publications than, The Sunday Times, Northern Echo, The Field, Birmingham Gazette, Nottingham Journal, The Globe, Yorkshire Post, Daily Herald, Daily Express, Athenaeum, The Studio, Graphic, Evening Standard, The Queen, Newcastle Weekly, Outlook, The Architect, Jewish Guardian, Ladies Pictorial and the Pall-Mall Gazette. Even more remarkable was the length of these reviews, which totalled 133 column inches. Today such an exhibition would be lucky to net three column inches. There were 91 works exhibited and eighteen were by non-members.

In The Architect, December issue Eric Gill wrote on the aims of the new art and the Society, which he helped to form. "A number of artists practising the art of wood engraving have formed themselves into a Society for the purposes of holding exhibitions from time to time.

Membership of the Society is confined to those who use the European method of wood engraving. This method, distinguished from the Japanese or Eastern method by the fact that prints are obtained by means of the printing press, is more suitable to the tradition and temperament of European artists, and is of greater utility in connection with book production and decoration.

Decoration (a word formerly always prefixed by the word ' mere ') is now returning to its right place at the head of artistic activities. In a decoration the artist is forced to consider the actual beauty of his work, and only secondly the beauty of the story or scene depicted. And as the bootmaker, however useful he may be as a voter, is as a workman primarily a maker of footwear, so the artist, however useful he may be as a story-teller is, as an artist, primarily a maker of things of beauty and not things of sentiment.

The modern world has been led to attach an absurd value to mere representation, and to judge all works from a mere imitation of natural form. There is, however, at the present time, by the mercy of God, a tendency to realise again the intrinsic value of works of art as opposed to their extrinsic or sentimental value, and, in this matter, wood engraving is especially valuable, from the exact imitation of nature, which, in paint or etching is comparatively easy and natural, is, in wood engraving, both difficult and unnatural. The wood engraver is forced by his material to have some respect for the thing in itself and to place an absolute value upon the art of drawing".

The press seized on the essentials of this exhibition. In the prints there was no stylistic trace of Bewick, only a distant technical link of the white line. There was no trace of the Japanese influence, it was European in design. And design was dominant. Cheap artist prints had arrived at a price that could be afforded by the public. The public can always afford prints but the style never seems to match their requirements.

The press scene was enlivened by another exhibition which coincided with the Society of Wood Engravers. Colnaghi's Galleries had opened a show of the work of the French engraver Auguste Lepere. This was too good for the critics to miss. A hammer blow came from the Jewish Guardian, "Let them examine the earlier (and best) work of Auguste Lepere now on exhibition elsewhere and they will see what free and expressive work was done by him (and many others) on lines which they have been taught to despise". Lepere's nearest follower in the S.W.E. was Gwendolen Raverat. The Globe hit them for going the wrong way. "But Lepere's woodcuts are in quite a different category, and can best be described as black and white wash drawings in three or four tones, executed with gusto upon wood, and rendered reproductive by a finesse of wood engraving that is almost unique". The English wood engravers were not at all keen on wash drawings, they wanted to get as far away from that as possible. The ghost of the Victorian commercial engraver was too close in time. Frank Rutter in the Sunday Times misses an opportunity. He says, "Quite latterly, however, and especially since the war, woodcuts have again sprung into popularity as a means of original artistic expression. England has had no such recognised leader among wood engravers as France possessed in the late Auguste Lepere, an important exhibition of whose etchings, woodcuts and lithographs is now open at Colnaghi's Galleries". The English leaders to achieve world renown at a later date were all in the first S.W.E. exhibition, but they were all virtually young men. Too young for Rutter. Lepere was trained by an English wood engraver called Smeeton. Smeeton could in no way have anticipated the fundamental changes which were to take place in Twentieth Century art. Stylistically Lepere was due to be eclipsed by the revolution which was then well under way in France and in England. He was at that time of very mature age. His work was naturalistic, academic and heavily influenced by French Impressionism, although it was very sensitive, fluid, lively and extremely skilful. But it was the same kind of skill which had brought etching and the academies into disrepute. The skill, when divorced from meaning grows cold. The critics at that time had not quite grown used to the fact that the world of Impressionism and that of Lepere were already by-passed. These young artists in this exhibition had made a very clean break. This does not often happen in English art affairs. The search for form, which is the research for fundamental expression, was through the design process with a strong emphasis on individuality.

The incorruptible Charles Marriott in his review in "Outlook" is not at all clear in his outlook, and he sits uncomfortably on the fence as obtuse as ever, "No apology is needed for the above heading (Plain and Coloured) because, like most sayings which have been worn by use, it contains a profound truth: that colour in art is a glorious "extra" and not a necessity.

This is to clear the ground for the consideration of a sudden rush of black and white exhibitions. The very merits of the first annual exhibition of the Society of Wood Engravers.... provoke a melancholy reflection, followed, however, by a hope of something beyond art as it is commonly understood. The melancholy reflection is that we have come to a state in which artists are driven to seize as an opportunity what their forefathers regarded as a limitation. They have learnt to kiss their chains. No praise of the woodcut can conceal the fact that it is a more difficult way of doing something that could be done easily. The statement will probably be contested, but it is true, nevertheless, that with the mechanical means of reproduction at our disposal an ink drawing will achieve all that our forefathers aimed at in the woodcut. This, however does not condemn the modern revival of woodcutting; on the contrary, it puts it on a much higher plane than that claimed by the modern woodcutters themselves". The dirge continues and the first stage in the print revolution was staring the critics in the face. Jaundice is apt to infect writers in Fleet Street and cramp inspiration. The provincial press reaction was quite different. And here we have the younger journalist, learning his trade and heading for the Street. They appeared much more sure of their own judgments. The Northern Echo had a good contact with Eric Gill and states, "From some ' Notes ' I have received from Mr. Eric Gill, it appears that the old art of wood engraving is entering a new period of importance. Several artists practising wood engraving have formed themselves into a society, and their first exhibition is to be held at the Chenil Galleries. Mr. Gill believes that "by the mercy of God" the modern world is being weaned from the absurd practice of judging all art from a mere imitation of natural form, and is showing a tendency to realise again the intrinsic value of works of art as opposed to their extrinsic or sentimental value. It looks as if the first exhibition will be startling". By all accounts it was. The Birmingham Gazette anticipated the occasion and said, "The Society of Wood Engravers must be congratulated on their first exhibition at the Chenil Gallery. With such superb new examples of the old art as are shown here, there should follow a revival of public appreciation of this method of graphic expression". They were right in their forecast. In time public appreciation was to extend far beyond the country of its birth. The Yorkshire Post correspondent wrote, "... and the first annual exhibition opens to the public on Monday. For many years there has been a growing interest in the graphic arts. Various processes of engraving has been revived by artists as a medium for expression, commencing with etching, under the leadership of Sir Seymor Haden, and including, more recently, the formation of the Society of Graver Printers in Colour, whose remarkable achievements were recently noted in 'The Yorkshire Post'. Now comes this new society, the members of which restrict their practice to the use of wood blocks, either by cutting with a knife on the plank, or by engraving with a burin on the end grain of the box wood block. The young artists design their woodcuts and cut the blocks themselves.

Woodcutting is the oldest of the engraving processes, and goes back in Europe to about 1400. The present exhibition at Chelsea proves that new ideas in art can find adequate expression in the old medium. The wood engravers have a future, it is certain, and they have begun well". The Yorkshire Post was on the ball, which was to roll at a great speed and distance and later to embrace all the print media.

The 1921 exhibition saw a strengthening of the ranks and the new talents of Orovida, Hester Sainsbury and Paul Nash. Paul Nash exhibited three wood engravings, "Path through the Woods", "Snow Scene" and "The dark pool". All three prints were in editions of fifty prints and priced at one guinea each. He started his experiments in engraving in 1918 and this resulted in his brother John Nash and Dickey taking to the burin in 1919. This group published their first work containing engravings in The Sun Calender for the Year 1920. In 1921 Charles Ginner, Ethelbert White and Margaret Pilkington became members, and 1922 saw the election to membership of Paul Nash and Eric Dagleish. The sales figures for the 1921 exhibition realised £226.18.6. Members were however being advised and strongly recommended not to charge less than one guinea per print. Eric Gill met this request half way in 1921 show, with half at 10/6 and half at one guinea. In the 1922 minutes of the society there is an amusing entry. "Minimum price £1.1.0. per print subject to no serious objection from Mr. Gill". In the third annual exhibition catalogue the minimum price was one guinea, which included Eric Gill. 1922 also saw the first exhibition of the new engraving in Manchester, which was held in the Whitworth Institute Art Gallery and a second exhibition was planned for Oxford. The policy to actively promote the development of print beyond the confines of London, distinguishes this society from the others and this policy has been pursued into the present time. To do this, especially over a long period there must be continual development, by leading artists who are also blessed with more energy than is usual. There has never been any money behind them or available for this kind of public relations promotion. It has all been carried out solely on the basis that the work has been sent where it is wanted. Exhibitions were soon to appear in the north, south and east in this country and many countries overseas. For a very long time now very few art exhibitions ever travel to the West country. The early pioneers of the relief print development had this faith in their work and in the public's interest in what they were doing and the expansive scale of the present day print development has proved them right.

In the fourth 1923 exhibition held at the St. Georges Gallery, 32a George Street, Hanover Square, Claughton Pellew and John J.A. Murphy are the new engravers on the scene and the former was elected a member. Item 102 in the catalogue is entitled "Ten Woodcuts" by Paul Gauguin, priced at £80 set of 10. We will never see those prices again. Exhibitions in the provinces were continuing and the S.W.E. achieve their first overseas exhibition at the Carnegie Institute at Pittsburg. A second exhibition in 1924 was held at the Whitworth Institute Art Gallery and one at Southport. The public were still maintaining their support by buying 145 prints in 1923 and 178 prints at the 1924 annual exhibition. The society was then showing at the Redfern Gallery when the Gallery was in Arcade House, 27 Old Bond Street.

1925 was an eventful year in artist print history. A new society, known as the English Wood Engraving Society had been formed. A splinter group from the original society had resigned, and this move coincided with the change over of the older society from the St. Georges Gallery to the Redfern Gallery. This kind of move always wrenches existing loyalties and opens the way for dissension. There was however trouble in the camp, which appears to have been led by Edward Gordon Graig. With him went Claughton Pellew and Ethelbert White. Ginner resigned however because he was no longer engraving. The new society arranged its first exhibition at the St. George's Gallery to coincide with the original society then showing at the Redfern Gallery. To say the least it was not playing cricket. The Morning Post had this to say, "The Society of Wood Engravers had lost their Prince, Mr. Gordon Craig, who has resigned, and, with the assistance of two or three henchmen, formed the English Wood Engraving Society, the first exhibition of which was noticed in the Tuesday's "Morning Post".

"If the members of the elder body do not seem to miss their Hamlet, those of us who admire Mr. Craig's delightful art regret his defection, in spite of the many fine engravings on view at the Redfern Gallery." Later in 1938 he was awarded the R.D.I. by the Royal Society of Arts. He was an early recipient of this very coveted honour. The S.W.E. reaction to this splinter group is summed up in an entry in the November minutes, "It was resolved that the Society of Wood Engravers shall observe a friendly attitude towards the new Society". However the English Wood Engraving Society introduced some new talent including J.F. Greenwood, Frank Medworth, Alan Mc Nab, Margaret Greg, Dorothy Hirst, Leon Underwood and Blair Hughes-Stanton. Of these engravers and print makers Leon Underwood and Blair Hughes-Stanton were to prove major talent and later to make distinguished contributions to the art of engraving. They were creative artists who were not evolving out of illustration traditions. The Society of Wood Engravers also introduced new talent, Margaret Haythorne, Muriel Jackson, Eric Ravilious, David Jones, John Farleigh and Hesta Sainsbury. Eric Ravilious, David Jones and John Farleigh were to make a brilliant contribution to the history of engraving. In the 1925, S.W.E. exhibition Eric Gill and Paul Nash could still be purchased at one guinea, but no works were priced below this figure.

What was not generally realised at that time was that the German Bauhaus started in 1919 in Weimar. During the early Twenties Wassily Kandinsky, Lyonel Feininger, Gerhard Marchs, Lothar Schreyer, Leopold Survage and Walther Klemm were all masters at the Bauhaus and they were experimenting with the woodcut and wood engraving forms and techniques. Their approach was quite different from the English and French developments. Each group in the three countries were working on this revival independently of, and quite unknown to each other. Also when the works are studied together three separate form schools, all clearly defined, become an historical fact. No such exhibition has yet been staged, which would demonstrate these three schools of graphic form, but there is always hope for one in the future. There is however one common demoninator between the English and French groups, they were both composed of indigenous nationals whereas at the Bauhaus the group consisted of such diverse nationals as Russian, American, Austrian, Swiss, Hungarian and some Germans. They did however have a common object which was the analysis of the artists' language, which was to lead to the establishing of pure abstract forms. They even carried this abstract concept into the world of illustration and books. The Bauhaus Group, later, was to achieve a major and world wide implications and influence. This approach at that time was an anathema to the English artist and the public and it was also in direct opposition to the French group. The French have for a very long time based their abstraction upon the progressive reduction of visual reality, which they were prepared to develope to extreme limits, but never losing sight of the point of departure. Because of the fundamental standpoint of these two concepts, the French resisted the Bauhaus influence, until in the end they too had to accept and absorb it. The English group also was stylistically independent and was clearly based upon represent-ational images, springing from our literary and idiosyncratic poetry traditions and eclectic approach to abstraction, which was applied sparingly and sensitively, more as a stricture of form arising from the process of engraving itself. The English artist is not always articulate in abstract form and in very many cases confusion arises in their work. Continental artists and critics often charge the English in art as too often failing to drive an aesthetic home, sink or swim. In art the English like their form sublimated. Possibly this has something to do with scale. If the scale in art and architecture for that matter is carefully modulated to the human scale then people seem to be happy. Reduce the scale enormously by photography, then people will be even more happy, but confront them with the actual large scale work then they often want to attack it. The scale of modern engraving in wood is very large compared with pre-revolution work. Wide and open black space was a new experience, it had a high shock value and it resulted from the engravers' design policy or vision. Critics and people wanted this element sublimated, modulated and decorated. But the engravers took no notice, they were intent on driving the form aesthetic home and many succeeded in doing this.

Iain's first wood engraving to be exhibited in London was entitled "Winter" *Fig. 23* and it appeared at the Royal Society of Painter Etchers and Engravers at the R.W.S. Galleries in Conduit Street. He had already been an associate since 1923, during which time he had been showing etchings and drypoints. Later, however he did take up and experiment for a few years with lithography. When I asked him why he gave up lithography, he said, "It is really a pure drawing medium and very facile. I do not like it, because I am an engraver and one can do nothing with the stone".

In 1928 he was exhibiting with the Society of Wood Engravers in the London exhibition with four works "A Zeeland Port", "La Lessive", "Veere Harbour" and "La Lecon" along with the new talent of Clifford Webb and Clare Leighton. At the Society of Wood Engravers show at the Whitworth Art Gallery, Manchester he exhibited "The Canal, Annecy" *Fig. 8*, "Mont Blanc" and "The Mirror". The Birmingham Post described Iain's print as, the curiously complicated and elaborate "Zeeland Port", and the Sunday Times listed him as noteworthy. He was already well established as an outstanding draughtsman. In 1929 he exhibited the now famous print "Le Quai de Isle, Annecy", "A village in Savoy", "Le Sporting Bar" *Figs. 13 & 24* and "Le Gouter" at the S.W.E. exhibition. Frank Rutter in the Sunday Times commented, "Among the non-members exhibiting with this older Society Mr. Iain Macnab is a prominent contributor with four admirable prints among which ' Le Quai de Isle, Annecy ' is most effective in its bold, clear-hewn design and brilliant effect of light and shade." We also find Guy Malet's first wood engraving "An Irish Village" in this show, which was the same year that he became Iain's pupil at the Grosvenor School of Modern Art. This was quick work. In 1925 he had taken up the Principalship of this school and moved into 33 Warwick Square. From this time onwards each year his new work was shown at both societies, the R.E.s and the S.W.E. He also continued to show some works with the S.W.E. breakaway society the English Wood Engraving Society. This society became defunct in 1932, and as a result the Society of Wood Engravers gained some of their members and particularly Agnes Miller Parker, Gertrude Hermes, and Blair Hughes Stanton.

Iain's interest in people extends to more art societies. Although Edward Gordon Craig had left the Society of Wood Engravers, he was however training his son Edward Carrick to engrave. In 1929 Carrick formed a new print group and called it the Grubb Group. He adopted the motto "Ars Longa Grub Fugit". This light heartedness appealed to Iain, as artists on the whole take themselves too seriously, and especially in their attitudes towards the public. The Grubb Group shows were held at the Quo Vadis Restaurant in Dean Street, Soho. Iain added a further motto to this group, which was "Taste and See! Eat and Buy". They were anxious to give young artists a chance, and they only charged one shilling as hanging fee. The group continued until approximately 1931, but the idea of such exhibitions have continued to the present time.

After the first appearance of the wood engravings there would appear to be no production record of him continuing with the copper techniques of etching and drypoint. At this stage excepting for some lithography and lino-cuts he gives up his previous mediums which were all virtually limitless in technical range. He suddenly gives up all this freedom of the previous media for a medium which he describes in his book "The Students Book of Wood Engraving", 1938 as "Wood engraving had been under a cloud since the ' Nineties ', and had been looked upon as a rather old-fashioned method of reproducing drawings, and not as a form of artistic self-expression. Its very severity as a medium, however, gives it more scope for formal design: and this quality, along with its unexploited possibilities and very definite limitations, made it all the more attractive to those artists who were affected by the contemporary trend towards clarity and simplicity of statement, more clean-cut and precise draughtsmanship, and greater insistence on design." This was one of the reasons why Iain chose "to kiss the chains that bound them." (Charles Mariott). There were however further reasons for Iain's switch from etching to wood engraving, which can be seen in his drawings. Here he was really developing the power of expression from a greater economy of means. The most significant aesthetic statements of form are always compressed and concentrated. And to arrive anywhere near this kind of compressed experience the image has to be drawn. Even if today it is fashionable to devalue the role of drawing, then the previous statement still stands. And here lies the prize and real freedom. It is in the artist's hands and not in gimmicks.

Iain had set himself on a determined and straight course to the freedom arising from restriction. In some way this is similar to the difference between the athlete and the circus artist or performer. Through training the athlete will gradually work up to a climax of achieving a record, yet the circus artist must hold this pitch and fine balance in every performance that is undertaken. He is the greater artist because he has the freedom of a restricted discipline, which enables him to take over where the athlete may rest content. Igor Stravinsky described the paradox in his statement in Poetics in Music, "My freedom thus consists in my moving about within the narrow frame that I have assigned myself for each one of my undertakings. I shall go even further: my freedom will be so much the greater and more meaningful the more narrowly I limit my field of action and the more I surround myself with obstacles. Whatever diminishes constraints diminishes strength. The more constraints one imposes, the more one frees one's self of the chains that shackles the spirit."

The early thirties were vital years for the engraver and print maker. A print revolution was gaining momentum and was now well under way. John Buckland Wright, Joan Hassall and Gwenda Morgan had arrived on the engraving scene. John Buckland Wright left this country and became a very famous engraver in Belgium and France. When the Germans overran France during the second war he came back to this country and exercised an important influence in engraving and in teaching. This famous artist on landing in this country had to report to the Ministry of Labour to be allocated a war job. They asked him his occupation and he told them that he was an artist. The reply was "We have hundreds of those. Report to the camouflage department".

In 1932 Iain was invited to join the Society of Wood Engravers. He accepted the invitation and this society remained perhaps his most favoured Society throughout his life. This was because this Society continued to promote the art over and above just holding an annual exhibition. The S.W.E. were sending exhibitions to the provinces and overseas, and they continued to be the only Society to actively promote the development of the private press, limited edition book. This is a tradition which is carried on today with the same keenness and vigour. 1929 and 1930 saw the first two exhibitions of lino cuts in colour at the Redfern Gallery. The art of the lino cut is an extension of the art of engraving in a much softer material. This was however the beginnings of the fully developed colour print as we know it today. During the thirties the book publisher was beginning to show interest in engraving and the artists were equally interested in not only illustrating books, but starting a new era in book production by designing them and furthermore producing them as works of art in their own right. These books, all very limited editions are generally referred to as the kid glove book. When they are laid on their spines and sensitively opened they are expected to squeak. This arises from the leather hinges built into the spines.

Iain's first private press book, with an edition of 170 copies was "Nicht at Eenie. The Bairns Parnassus", which was published in 1932 by the Samson Press. The Samson Press was established in 1930 and run by J.M. Shelmerdine and Flora Grierson at Stuarts Hill Cottage, Warlingham, Surrey. This book contains 48 wood engravings as illustrations to childrens rhymes. The rhymes were collected by Dr. A.A.W. Ramsey. Most of the rhymes were sent by people who had heard them in the nursery and many of their sources are now untraceable. The engravings were designed to marry with a Goudy Modern type face and they comprise mainly head and tail pieces. *Fig. 6.* His interpretation of the childrens poems is vigorous, simple and witty and the style is based upon the use of the cut out shape and sharp silhouette. This his first illustrated book was followed in 1934 by Tam O Shanter from the Samson Press and was set in a Goudy Modern type face in an edition of 250 copies and is the tale by Robert Burns. Here the Scottish character, tradition and wit is happily married in the combination of these two Scottish artists. This book is very different from the first in that the thirteen engravings are all based upon head piece design, and each retaining their essential rectangular shape *Figs. 35, 36 & 37* shows Iain's masterly characterisation of the individual Scots types and each form is engraved with an outstanding economy of the burin.

By this time the engravers knew where they were going. The private press book had a slow start from about 1924. Then Robert Gibbings starts up the Golden Cockerel Press. He was working in collaboration with Eric Gill and produced many works which were masterpieces of great importance, which culminated in the Golden Cockerel's "Four Gospels." (1931) with 41 engravings by Gill and set in Gill's Golden Cockerel type face. Later most of the engravers produce one or many Golden Cockerels. The general publisher was also becoming interested in the way engraving was developing. In 1932 Constable and Company produced the astonishing and refreshing book by George Bernard Shaw, "The Adventures of the Black Girl in her search for God". This book, which was a landmark and illustrated by 20 wood engravings from John Farleigh. John Farleigh's illustrations at the time received far more publicity than G.B.S. and G.B.S. was not very pleased about it. Around the mid-thirties Penguin Books Ltd. (Allen Lane) began publishing a series of paper backed Penguin Illustrated Classics. Robert Gibbings was appointed Art Editor of the series and Iain produced the Illustrated Classic "Selected Poems of Robert Browning" in 1938 which contained 16 wood engravings. Iain's engraving by this time had become more fluid. *Fig. 5* and indeed Browning inspired him to produce romantic work. This is where both author and illustrator should be in sympathy. In this case the art editor knew all his engravers very well. Iain's finest book from the private press is "The Sculptured Garland". It contained 16 wood engravings and was published in 1948 by the Dropmore Press of Great Ormond Street, London. An edition of three hundred copies were printed, using a 14 point Monotype Garamond type face. The book is a selection from the Lyrical Poems of Walter Savage Landor which were chosen and arranged by Richard Buxton and the bindings are by Evans of Croydon. In *Fig. 3* we can see his sensitivity as a designer in the manner in which he relates and balances the engraving with the type setting. The whole has a sculptural character and gravity, quite different from any of his previous works. On the selection of the poems Richard Buxton brings the sculptural literary qualities forward when he write in his preface, "This is in fact a garland and for the choice of the flowers and their weaving together the editor is responsible. But in the weaving he has sought to bear in mind that precision and purity of Landor's line which have made the word 'sculptural' inevitable." Iain's interpretation of these sculptural and linear qualities complete the book as a work of art. Some of the engravings are expansive whole pages and the rest are head pieces. "The Graces" *Fig. 9* with the enclosing sharply cut line at the top and the open free line at the bottom is also a good example of the figure draughtsman in engraving. The whole is rhythmically free and sculptural: a perfectly classical composition and carried out with a masterly economy of means. There is not a single superfluous line in the work.

The thirties and forties were the heyday of the kid glove book, both in this country and in France with the history making Vollard productions. In the meantime Christopher Sandford had taken over the Golden Cockerel Press and in 1948 in his "Cockaloram" he talks of the 181 books published by the press. The other outstanding private presses were the Gregynog Press, Kynoch Press and the Nonesuch Press. Hitler's war was ultimately responsible for the total eclipse of the private press book. The whole idea of a private press book is an anachronism in as much as it is a book which very few people can afford to buy. It also represents a quality of production which cannot yet be achieved with all the resources of science behind the development of the commercial presses. Secondly if the commercial presses were to attempt this quality of production not enough people would be found to support such a project. This also now applies to the artist colour print, which have been marketed in large unlimited editions at relatively low prices, but with the wide open public there is not enough demand. This also gives the answer to Gill's creed of his 10/6 prints, which now sell much easier at £160. The glory of the private press book is in the fact that they enshrine a large body of fine engraving by a team of engravers the like of which we are never likely to see repeated, and many of them demonstrated the raising of fine book production into the realm of fine art. And whatever value we may place on craft today, we shall never attain their equal unless we also are able to achieve the level of craftsmanship of these committed men and women. Today there is even some dispute as to what a professional artist is. Well the previous statement on craft is one of the basic requirements. Recently Enid Marx R.D.I., F.S.I.A., F.R.S.A. said to me "It is tragic to see the lack of craft in the work of the younger generation. Craft is after all an essential quality if these young artists are to become professional."

In Chapter 2 a sharp distinction is drawn between the techniques of illustration and art. The whole of the world of print has its origins in illustration. A dominant aspect of this world is the demands made by the book, which introduces a set of conventions arising from the manner in which a book is read. Because of this long standing tradition it is natural for the early engravings to be heavily influenced by the illustration techniques. Also the elimination of them must be an aim and the process takes a long time. The end result of freedom from these strictures must be seen well ahead of the actual production at the time. Our engravers did however persist in the pursuit of the Noel Rooke concept of evolving a design structure out of the inherent characteristics of the burin and boxwood and to this we must now also include the lino cut on softer material as a variation of engraving. The logical development of such a basic concept, must if carried out to the letter, eventually arrive at a state of aesthetic purity. On this pursuit not a single engraver let up. Engraving and the world of print, as a direct result was a continually evolving process. And it was around this time that the autonomous print was to evolve. That is a print, self contained with complete technical development which in its own right stands on its own merits as a unique work of art. These engravers had already achieved this in the private press book. Engravings were also getting larger as time progressed and the early stiffness of technique was now giving way to a mature fluidity. This brought forth an interesting reflection from the critic of the Sunday Times, who in December 1935 remarked on the Society of Wood Engravers at the Redfern Gallery, "In black and white art, British artists are supreme, and wood engraving, especially, provides them with plentiful opportunities for interesting techniques. The very materials used demand a degree of application and control which puts the artists on their mettle, and a British wood engraving carelessly produced as to its craftsmanship would almost rank as a curiosity. Black and white, again, besides having a dignity, vigour, and wholesomeness of their own, whether in pictures or women's dress, can suggest, by subtle degrees of tone, and contrast, a wealth of colour to sensitive minds." The curiosity of bad craftsmanship is always weeded out of exhibitions by the selection commit-tees and in this case it was Robert Gibbings and Agnes Miller Parker. With this pair of engravers bad craftsmanship would not stand a chance. Gui St Bernard in January 1937 in "Coming Events" also makes further observations on the engravers' progress. "It is often said that British people are at their best when expressing themselves in simple terms. Our artists, for example, can claim world-leadership in the use of black and white media, especially wood engraving. This is not to imply that they cannot use colour or other complicated means, or that every print they produce is an unchallengeable masterpiece. It is, rather, that the very limitations of black and white, and the consequent necessity for careful distillation of ideas, raise just the problems which put British artists on their mettle.

The last twenty years or so have seen a remarkable revival of wood engraving, as an independent form of pictorial art even more than in the illustrative sense. It is true that the increasing numbers of limited edition books produced in recent years have provided artists who for long have been ousted by purely mechanical processes, with the opportunities to exercise their skill, as did their forerunners of bygone ages, on illustrations which are something more than mere adjuncts to stories. But the outstanding point is the extent to which wood engravings have become accepted as pictures, to be framed and hung in the ordinary way."

Iain had played a major role both as producer and teacher in the ultimate emancipation of the pure art of engraving. During the thirties he had produced many autonomous prints including such works as the well known examples as the "The Waterfront, Calvi, Corsica 1930" *Fig. 25,* "Corsican Landscape 1931" *Fig. 26,* "Southern Landscape 1933" *Fig. 28,* "Two Fat Ladies 1936" *Fig. 30* and "Drying Sails, Lake Garda 1938" *Fig. 31.* His print production for the 1940s is naturally small. Hitler's war had intervened, and service in the Royal Air Force had swallowed up five more years to which must be added the time spent in hospitals recovering from war wounds. He was in and out of hospital very many times before he died. One day during the 60s I met him after another session in hospital and said, "Hello Iain how are you." He replied "Oh, I am well now. They have patched me up. Each time things get better because there is nothing left for them to cut away now."

However busy the surgeons had been cutting him away piece by piece, he pushed this aside and continued cutting away at his boxwood blocks. With the book "The Sculptured Garland" behind him, he continued to develop the pure engraving and in the 50s and 60s he brought all his art, technical ability and experience together in a glorious run of prints. It is something of a mystery to me, that despite his precarious physical health, having cheated death so many times, that he was able to achieve the magnificent last run of the final period, without, in his work giving away the slightest sign of being physically below par. Engraving is after all a very physical process, requiring strength and an intensely high power of concentration. In fact his powers of concentration increased right up to the last composition "Ronda Bridge, Spain" 1961 *Fig. 34.* This print represents the full power of the black and white element concentrated in a manner he had not achieved previously, the pure white line is used with an absolute architectural economy and the textures which are linear are some of the most sensitive ever to be produced in engraving. This one print has everything that Iain was in engraving. It could not have been produced by any other person. I also at this point marvel at his wisdom, for it is of great importance for a significant artist to know which work should rightly be his last. How does one know? After all he lived into 1967. He also did a very impressive painting after the production of the engraving of the same bridge. Many times I asked if there were any more engravings on the way, and he would say, "No, my eyesight is not good enough." It is of course a well known fact that eyesight brings an engraver to an end long before they are affected in any other medium. This is easily understandable optically, but then optical instrumental assistance can be applied to keep an engraver at work for an extended period. But, no, Iain did not want this optical assistance. He was of course physically weak during the last few years, but not to the extent that more works were impossible. The answer is I feel given in a discussion we shared on this engraving, he said, "It is my largest work. You know as I do that it has all that we know engraving to be. It is my signature to the cheque. Now I have decided not to risk a failure." This was an aspect of Iain's wisdom, or foresight or knowledge. He had made yet another clear cut decision, his last performance, as with the circus artist, had to be his best.

The engravers so far introduced into this book form a distinct School of British Engraving, the quality and completeness of which has no equal. From this point of view the present list is not by any means complete, in that it does not include the younger generations. A School as such is as complete an entity as is the Norwich School of Painting, and in this country we have had only this one with which to boast. Our second School, that of engraving will eventually be seen as both larger and more important in its import than the Norwich School. Such a concept has never been researched and developed critically, and many of those engravers forming the School are still living. This gap in our critical world is controlled by the editors of newspapers and their policies. It is simple, if the editorial policy is to go this or that way, then you the critic will be paid only if you can supply what we the editors want. In these matters my experience is more than sufficient to support the statement. We also seem to produce very few critics of book production calibre. Because of this editorial policy set up the School of Engraving becomes a critical accident for the simple reason that they were opening up two fields at the same time, the autonomous print, illustration and the artist produced book. Critics because of their personal prejudice and controlling editorial policy either cover art or illustration, but usually not both, and certainly not the development of illustration into art. Because of this there is virtually little coverage at all unless it is an exhibition, and if it is not an exhibition then it cannot be news, and if it is not news, you the critic just must not touch it. Hence the critical accident. The engraving phenomenon, which is now our great heritage found its way into the development of the private press book with very limited editions, and the work in many of these books is not illustration at all in the strict sense, but art with a big A. A large body of our top level art production in engraving is enshrined in these glorious volumes, which are mostly in private libraries, and today many people and students, who should know these works have not even seen them, and many have not even heard of them. If these works are ever exhibited they can only be shown open at one page. Also if any person needs to study them then their scale virtually demands at least one day per book and each book is a closed exhibition itself.

For a school of aesthetic development to exist as such there must be the essential qualifications which will enable artists to work individually on a common cause or concept. I have previously, though briefly sketched in the existence of clear cut German and French Schools of Engraving and are well documented. The British School of Engraving is equally clear cut in philosophy, aims, form development and stylistic character. This is where Bewick and William Blake step into the picture. Firstly these artists sparked off the white line technical concept. A black line concept could equally well have caught the imagination and become an aim, but it did not and so far has not. All the British engravers are in the white line tradition and development to a man and woman. Secondly there is the common concept which was the Rooke design philosophy to find a design structure that would evolve naturally from the act of engraving with a burin. This design development is there in all the engravers for all to see. It is not for nothing that British engraving is considered some of the finest in the world. Thirdly a common concept of the autonomous print evolved eventually and later in most of the mentioned engravers production. The autonomous print had to evolve from the world of illustration and other well enumerated techniques. Until the autonomous print had arrived there was no way of assessing the full potential of engraving.

Jean Jean Jean.
Figure 6 — *Illustration from Nicht at Eenie, the Bairn's Parnassus. 1932*

Figure 7 — *Landscape near Cassis 1930*

Figure 8 — *The Canal. Annecy 1928*

Figure 9 –   *The Graces. 1948*

Figure 10 –   *Gathering Wood. 1947*

Figure 11 —   *The Brave Bull. 1951*

Figure 12 —   *Las Lavanderas. 1936*

Figure 13 — *Le Sporting Bar. 1929*

Figure 14 — *Picking Pyrethrum. Kenya 1957*

Figure 15 — *The Mews at night. (33 Warwick Square) 1954*

Figure 16 — *Cassis. 1933*

Figure 17 — *The House Opposite. 1950*

Figure 18 — *Portuguese Shipyard. 1959*

Figure 19 — *Gossip. Corsica 1950*

Figure 20 — *The Back Gardens. Lisbon 1959*

Figure 21 — *River in Spate. 1960*

Figure 22 — *The Fallen Willow. 1949*

4 - Drawing, the dividing line

Drawing is one of the most abstract of all aspects of art. It starts with a simple, but pregnant dot. A dot can be brought to life and extended into a line. As soon as a line is drawn, thought, feeling and emotion are on the road to expression. A line can be long or short, straight or curved, thick or thin, pure form or formless, wet or dry, fast or slow, sharp or rough, vibrating or taut, strong or weak, sensitive or crude, staccato or flowing, lost or found, hesitant or determined, accurate or inaccurate, awkward or articulate, erudite or illiterate, mechanical or erratic, static or dynamic, dividing or enclosing, inhibited or extrovert, cut or eroded and adult or infantile. Such is the orchestral range. There is however one purpose that drawing does not serve so well, and that is imitation and naturalism. Granted there are worlds of naturalistic illustration where imitation is the objective, but this field does not come within the range of this book.

Drawing is the most fundamental forming process at the artist's disposal. All the significant artists of this century and any other for that matter are all fine draughtsmen. Iain viewed drawing as design and wrote the following statement, "All drawing is, of course, design. When an artist draws from the figure he is simply designing in terms of solid and linear forms. To have any value, his design must express his reactions. On these reactions depends the merit of the drawing." Iain's reactions to form were clearly expressed in his own work in a consistent progression through his life time.

Every human being in very early life draws, as he or she must, before even writing can begin. The child must draw to communicate even if he or she is not understood. Later letters must be formed to develop other means of communication and these must be drawn, up to a point where the shapes are memorised and the flow of free handwriting begins to develop. Free handwriting is a very pure form of expression. So much so that the bank manager still prefers to rely for identification upon a person's signature rather than a computer number. Finally an artist should arrive at a point where his form becomes his signature. But not many bank managers see the business potential of exchanging artists' drawings for cash. The development of the signature facility of self expression is sufficient for many people, and their ability to draw usually ceases at this point. A decision to give up drawing is further aided and abetted by the inevitable intrusion of three dimensional geometry and the first complications of the third dimension into the scheme of things. But many need much more than this, like the child quoted in an essay by Roger Fry, when asked how she produced her drawings, replied, "I think, and then I draw a line round my think". Form research begins at an early age. This child has said something very important about drawing and one of the outstanding characteristics of a child's drawing, apart from the infantile image is that in their work they are usually beautifully balanced between the intellect, what is said and ability, which is the manner in which the image is formed. A balance between the intellect and skill is critical throughout life, and the makings of a fine and significant draughtsman can only result from an intellect of a capacity capable of keeping the skill continually taut. From this standpoint an excess of skill and a sluggish intellect are bad companions for an artist. Landseer was a good example of too much talent and too little interest in form. His drawing of the dog, at the age of ten years, which so deservedly won The Royal Society of Arts Medal 1813, is purely illustrative, phenomenally skilful, and stamped at so early an age in the desired image of his time. He became a glorified illustrator, and only on very rare occasions, did form appear, then only in some of his drawings, and of birds in particular. Landseer as a child could not "draw a line round my think", he recorded only what he saw, not necessarily understanding or appreciating what he saw. A child today would certainly have something to say about a dog.

From the point, or dot and line we move very quickly into the whole gamut of human expression and communication. Drawing in some form or another is required throughout our lives from the infantile two dimensional images of extreme youth through to the expression of three dimensional experience and ultimately to the expression of the most profound thinking, which is now giving rise to the expression of four dimensional form. In this respect photography is of little help.

In any consideration of Iain as a draughtsman we must consider drawing as a fine art. It being thus a language and what is being said is of prime importance. He was essentially a figure draughtsman of a very high order. Top quality figure draughtsmen are always small in number in any country at one time. In time, production and importance he was running parallel with Eric Gill and Bernard Meninsky, both figure draughtsmen of high rank and achievement. As draughtsmen, Iain's form was expressed through an electrically energetic, taut line of exceptional economy, which was swift and certain to capture the volume and thrust within the form. Eric Gill's line was simple, unerring, refined and classically pedantic and surprisingly defined the shape only, and solids were suggested. Bernard Meninsky's line flowed freely as a river estuary expressing the joy of relaxed rythmns, and release, entwining in its progress the gravity of the volume of the form delineated. In this respect three distinctly different personalities have been described in terms of the way in which the line has been used and drawn. The subject, the human figure being common to all three, and indeed the technique of the simple pencil, brush and paper is common. Figure drawing as a subject for the exercise of form and aesthetic disciplines is very important. The human figure is still the most complex, subtle and dynamic form in front of which, the draughtsman can be tested. John Buckland Wright the engraver and figure draughtsman often said, "that the figure draughtsman is still a mark of the professional in art." His conception of the professional in art, meant a person so trained, organised and talented that he or she was capable of producing anything likely to be normally demanded of a trained artist. Today, we have an art form, where an ephemeral event or happening is produced instead of a physical work of art. The professional artist was a matter and concept with which Iain was very concerned and in his book "Figure Drawing" he states, "The artist's drawing, in fact, should be an index of his artistic status. It may be compared to a balance sheet and should show a true and complete state of his (aesthetic) affairs and capabilities at any given time.

When he is drawing, on the other hand, the last thing he should be thinking of is making a good drawing. He is solely concerned with the testing and the directing of his reactions." In fact a good drawing, in the finished sense is a drawing, killed and finished off or a dead duck. A drawing must therefore be a working drawing, a study up to a certain point, which is then a means to another end or interpretation into another medium. If it is a true working drawing it will have the quality of a complete statement, of aesthetic significance at whatever stage the draughtsman may leave it. In the same book he gives a clear statement on aims in drawing, "The artist takes the human figure as a model because there he will meet every problem which can be found in any branch of art. The main problem of the draughtsman in studying from life is to see the figure as a complete and vital design. When the artist speaks of the vitality or the life of a design, he means the life inherent in the design — a life which may have nothing at all to do with the human life which he sees in the model. He studies in order to increase his perception of that life. He trains himself to read it instinctively and to experience a pleasurable sensation in contemplating, not the model, but the aesthetic life and movement of the form. Unless the artist can see the figure as a design with every mass and line, whether bone, muscle or feature, as part of that design, and contributing to its life and unity, he will find himself attempting to copy the personal life of the model. But there he is bound to be defeated, as no copy of human life can ever be as alive as a living person. If he wishes to create a work of art he must abandon any idea of making a mere copy or description of the appearance of the model. He must search for some other kind of life in addition to and quite distinct from the human life of the model." Iain's aesthetic affairs and world of form expresses an unquestioned certainty and high aspiration. It is a world of strength and hope generously leavened with a richness of content and structure. He was like this as a man, and just his presence conveyed this air of authority and self assurance. His aesthetic judgment was sought by many and was always given freely. In his life time he made far less mistakes than most in art and his relationships with people. Such an objective is difficult to attain and it is a good position to be fired at and he was shot at from some critical quarters on several occasions. But the toughness of his line was also the toughness of the man. Like a spring he was back on equilibrium just as soon as the shot had hit. In strategy he was very rarely caught out, this quality is seen in his power of composition. Whether on a block, paper or canvas, or organising art and people. Every move was worked out well ahead of the event.

It is this life in addition to and quite distinct from the human model which has held its fascination for great minds through the centuries. Even in this scientific and technological age it is not beyond reason to still refer to these qualities of drawing as magic. We may well need another word other than magic or miracle to describe the astounding phenomenon of a man, with a simple point and few lines, summing up in a unique image, man's loftiest thoughts on form and space, to be preserved and cherished from one generation to another and handed down through the centuries. Iain and others have used the word magic in the same sense as in his own words he has said, "In all good drawing there is this pictorial life, this motive quality, this animation of line and mass — call it what one will. Perhaps magic is as good a word as any."

The student is on occasion in a position to both see and experience the magic or master-piece literally forming in front of his eyes. I remember this happening to me as a student at Camberwell School of Art when Sir Thomas Monnington, now the President of the Royal Academy sitting on my donkey, demonstrated alongside my drawing. He virtually glided very quietly into a comfortable position, talking aloud in a soft rythmical voice, apparently com-pletely relaxed, with the pencil lightly held between his sensitive fingers, which were surely and economically delineating the form of the model's head as he spoke. Every line was a pure authoritative abstraction. Some lines were emphasised and others sublimated in relation to space, but the relaxed form of this drawing, which evolved in front of my hungry eyes was as calm and erudite as was Tom Monnington on that morning. There are many students who have experienced such demonstrations from Iain's hand.

But this drawing phenomenon as a fine art is no prerogative of modern man. These qualities are also found in some of the earliest records of man in the caves of Altamira and Lascaux. In these caves are drawings of unsurpassed quality, produced by Paleolithic man some ten to twenty thousand years ago. The images are simple and are of the animals of the hunt and chase. These drawings have an amazing subtlety of observation, they are highly charged with dynamic linear energy, they also have a very real sense of gravity and movement and are pure aesthetic transcriptions of the animals identity and significance to the life of Paleolithic man. For us today to say they are symbols is not enough. Bernard Menninsky in his "The appreciation of drawing", which he wrote for the Arts Council 1948 exhibition catalogue entitled, "The art of drawing" got perhaps closer than anyone else in the Twentieth century writing on drawing, to some of the mysteries and magic of the art. "The act of artistic creation seems to be as mysterious and inaccessible as life itself. Indeed, were it to become known and logically demonstrable, it would cease to be art and become science. Creative values can never be proved, only felt.

In attempting the question we enter the domain of aesthetics. Here, however, we are in a vague, shifting world where few things are certain. Slowly, through the centuries, men have agreed on putting a high value on critically selected works of art. Attempts to explain their pre-eminence are without end. Ultimately, it would seem as though a great work of art is capable of absorbing and justifying all expositions of its greatness, whilst at the same time preserving its ineffable secret, holding within itself the power to engender fresh speculation and delight. The great draughtsman of all ages are men who have produced images of the drawn line, which hold within themselves the qualities necessary for their aesthetic significance and survival."

The drawn line is as abstract and pure as is music. Therefore when lines are brought together they must each of them have significance. All drawing is also an act of memory. When drawing a line on paper the draughtsman is no longer, during that time, viewing the model. The resulting image will be a mental one and a comment of some kind and an individual statement. The moving power in an artist's drawing is the recorded intensity of his vision. Even if there is a high fidelity to the strict three dimensional visual appearance the individuality will be stamped in every line. It is this individuality which gives aesthetic pleasure. Individuality and aesthetic value are equally apparent if the subject of the drawing is abstract. Individuality and aesthetic value were very important for Iain and his comments are pertinent. "When you make a drawing you are concerned with lines flowing through the picture — lines of force running along the picture — then you reduce about a third dimension. You look for any lines in the picture, which enable you to give life to the design. You may be drawing a house and you say there is no action in a house (unless there is an earthquake), but the lines which compose the contours of the house do have a certain amount of movement. You are deliberately projecting your sense of design or nature by looking for repetition of lines and patterns and stressing them.

The problem is a little more difficult when you have several figures instead of one. Obviously when I am making a composition I must have some kind of lines leading into the picture. If I stress the line and make it an important point of my design I must make sure that it is repeated somewhere else in the picture. It is only by over-statement that you can avoid under-statement — this is very important. This fuss about abstract art is not made about music — no one asks for a ' Symphony in Blue Major ' (one isn't expected in music, to produce exact images — people will expect it of artists — and oughtn't to). The artist has something to say, but it can only be said in terms of line, colour, tone and so on. You might say every picture is abstract from this stand point." Iain's drawings demonstrate that his means could not be more abstract. His line is calligraphic, at times almost Chinese and his drawings are virtually written.

A fine drawing gives a heightened sense of reality and the mind delights in unity. Unity can only be realised through intensive study and application. Given keen vision, trained perception and intuition the artist, through the forming process is then able to create a higher reality, or the idea behind the fact. The work is more like the subject than the thing itself. This aspect of art is also cumulative. The artist is bringing his experience forward and each work progresses until in maturity a single drawing can be charged with the meaning of a lifetime's experience. Time is layered and matrixed in a single drawing. In Chinese art cumulative experience and time expressed within a work is a standard of measure used by the senior master to judge the work of a junior master or that of a student. Chinese artists are usually of very mature years before being recognised as a master artist. If the artist has drawn one hundred melons, the last one must contain the experience of all that have preceded it. To achieve such a compression of time and experience with such a simple form, omission must play a major part in the discipline. The omission of all that is surplus, superficial and anecdotal is an aim common to the oriental and occidental artist, although the methods of achieving it are different. An oriental artist sublimates individualtiy and contributes to a continuity of unbroken tradition, whereas the occidental artist emphasises individuality, which dies with one and the continuity of tradition arises from the perpetual change over from individual contributors.

In many of the drawings illustrated Iain has used a paint brush, which is very unusual for a western draughtsman. The way in which the brush is used is a pure calligraphy. The pointed brush is also used in the same manner as the Chinese calligraphic artist. It is very rare indeed to see volume expressed with such force, thrust and gravity, with the delicate whip lash sensitivity of the sable brush. The economy of means embracing the total experience gives the observer the right amount and quality of visual information to enable him or her to complete the image. This is the powerful art of omission in which the Chinese excel.

These sharp qualities in his drawings met a very adverse critical response at a one man show he held at the Albany Gallery, Sackville Street in 1931. The critic in the Scotsman writes under the heading "Artistic slight of hand." "Again it is clear that Iain Macnab is a stylist, more concerned with the smart rendering of his subject than with the subject itself.... Macnab has made a large number of drawings clever to the verge of slickness, and has evidently enjoyed his own slight-of-hand prodigiously." R.H. Wilenski writing in the Observer gave another point of view, "Mr. Iain Macnab is an artist of natural liveness with a natural feeling for graphic style. Nothing that he does is therefore dull or commonplace. His work is invariably alive and invariably swagger.... Macnab uses pen or pencil for an elegant and rapid outline and then with a hog's hair brush he applies wash tones which provide further information and at the same time enrich the pattern on the page. The results remind me of drawings by certain Baroque masters whose bravura and assurance are qualities so rarely met with in the works of artists to today." The art critic of the Morning Post writes under the heading "Dangerous convention.... Mr. Iain Macnab has adopted a dangerous convention in his studies of the nude on view at the Albany Gallery. It is apt to lead to emptiness or partial over-emphasis, such as we see in the slickness, abnormal thighs and small heads.... Even decorative intention does not justify physical deformity of this dimension. In most of them inner content is sacrificed to more or less ponderous contours." Frank Rutter in the Sunday Times had this to say. "Another room is entirely filled with drawings from the life, and this exceedingly able and varied array of nude studies is valuable evidence of Mr. Iain Macnab's gifts and qualifications as a teacher. Almost every kind of drawing is included in this collection. Here are pen-drawings, fine and incisive in line, drawings in red chalk but subtle in modelling, and brush-drawing in which form is boldly hewn out in masses of light and shade. But whatever the instrument employed, the interpretation of form is intensely alive, and the drawing has the appearance of being spontaneous, profoundly sincere and intelligently sensitive. All have an air of great decision, betokening an artist who knows his mind, knows what he wants to do, and knows how to do it." The really important aspect of this critical response is the fact that these drawings were strong enough to split the critics into two camps. Often Iain has said that the very worst thing that can befall an artist is to be ignored.

The timeless profundity of drawing led Michaelangelo to place a supreme importance on drawing over and above the largest painted wall decorations. In de Hollanda's "Four Dialogues on painting." Michaelangelo says, "Let this be plain to all: design, or as it is called by another name, drawing, constitutes the fountain-head and substance of painting and sculpture and architecture and every other kind of painting, and is the root of all sciences. Let him who has attained the possession of this be assured that he possesses a great treasure; he will be able to make figures taller than any tower, both painted and as statues, and he will find no wall or side of a building that will not prove narrow or small for his great imaginings. He will be able to paint frescoes in the old Italian fashion, with all its usual mingling and variety of colours; he will be able to paint very smoothly in oil, with more skill, daring and patience than mere painters can; finally, in the scanty space of a piece of parchment he will prove himself a great and most perfect artist, as great as in those other ways. And because the power of design or drawing is great, so very great, Messer Francisco Hollanda can, if he choose, paint whatsoever he can draw." If we lost all the paintings and sculpture of Michaelangelo there would be everything that he is in the drawings at the British Museum. As Michaelangelo is to most people, everything there is in art, so in his work, everything is fused into a single whole. His drawings represent a maximum concentration of aesthetic experience. This quality is common to all the great master draughtsmen. The readability of such a compressed experience is made possible by rhythm. Without rhythm there is no movement from which a language can flow, an absence of rhythm implies an irregular measurement which will defeat understanding and no rhythm will negate development and cancel out content. There must be and there is rhythm in all things. Form without rhythm is outside of art.

Throughout his life and in all his activities Iain placed a high value on rhythm. He said, "We talk glibly of rhythm in art but few of us trouble to define exactly what we mean by rhythm. The Oxford Dictionary gives: "(Art) the harmonious correlation of parts," but this, if one may criticise so erudite a production, is rather begging the question. The same authority, however, becomes a little more precise when it says: "(Physics, Physiol, and gen) movement with regular succession of strong and weak elements."

Rhythm may be defined as repetition in an ordered sequence and its effect upon the human faculties is curiously emotive. From the earliest times rhythm has affected mankind profoundly in his beliefs, his arts and his every activity. It has caused him to attach a religious significance to the movements of the heavenly bodies, to the seasons of the year and to all the processes of nature. Under its sway he creates gods and makes magic. Even today, for all our sophistication, we are just as conscious of its emotive effect in all the arts.

By organising his lines and planes into ordered sequences the draughtsman invests his forms with emotional significance. A single line or plane by itself will have little or no meaning, although a curved line or surface will express a greater feeling of movement than one which is straight, due to the tendency of the eye to run along a curve. I have heard it contended that the inclination to the eye of a plane has a certain emotional quality, but this is very doubtful. It is true that if we repeat a line or a plane we obtain a simple harmony and it is not until this repetition becomes a rhythmical sequence in conjunction with other and contrasting sequences of a similar nature, that it can be in any way dynamic or expressive of an emotional experience. Divorced from its context no line or plane can have any more pictorial significance, than a note struck at random on the piano, or one of those little spots of colour found on a paint manufacturers circular.

Rhythm and curvature and their counterpoint have been important and consistent features of Iain's drawing and engraving. It forms a very important part of his aesthetic personality. Rhythm and curvature are as he says expressive of an emotional experience. In the art the Scots are more directly emotional than the English. This can be seen very clearly in Scottish painting. There are not very many Scottish engravers of Iain's quality for the purposes of making a comparison. In making these comparisons he would state with some feeling and Scottish pride that he and his countrymen in art were very much closer to Paris than London. The Parisian and London differences are real, in the degrees of the sublimation of emotion in the approach to form. French and Scottish art are both more sensuous and emotionally direct. And nothing in recent drawing could be more direct than the electrified speed and accuracy of Iain's line and particularly his curvature. Indeed in drawing there are few who could aim such long curves from beginning to the end with such unwavering certainity with the accuracy of a Bisley rifle marksman. Naturally in such expression there is no room for surface pimples or superficial surface craters, wavering or particular statements on minute details. The statement is generalised. A generalised statement in line can mean one or two things, a summing up of vast experience, or the emptiness of no or little experience. Iain's mind worked as fast as his line. Generalised form statements, summing up a situation are to some extent idealistic and thereby classical in nature. A classicist from this point of view being one who cannot take life as he finds it and in form sets out to recreate the world in an ordered fashion of his ideal mould.

The supreme example of classical form in this respect is Raphael who created the great calm. An ideal stillness of pure form orientated on the circle. Even the Raphaelian form concept of drawing was consistently based upon curvature. The curvature of line continued until the form of the figure was captured in a linear cage. But the cage expressed a graceful, rhythmical and flowing form life. There is also a generosity being expressed and a very firm confidence in the belief of goodness. In Iain's work this confidence never wavered. He believed in it as much as he believed in and felt the rhythms of life run through him and likewise in other people. Iain in fact loved the built in inevitability of rhythm and change in life. On many occasions he has said, "Thank God for change, it is man's only way out of his predicament." Within a state of continuous change however there is a point or centre of no change. It is four dimensional or space-time concept, where the conditions and structure for change can be firstly accommodated and secondly demonstrated. Rhythm and curvature in his work was always present. It was an important quality in his form and aesthetic structure. In his life's output this line ran straight. Only the subjects and media changed. It is only an artist of high calibre who can keep such a time line running straight. As a personality he was most generous to others, and as an artist in terms of pure form he had developed an aesthetic expression through which flowed the grace and generous comment on life. The rhythm determined the kind and degree of emotion. Classical qualities of this kind require a capacity for detachment, contemplation and synthesis.

The two main counter streams of drawing, which Iain had to contend with were the influences of the Bloomsbury School, based upon Cezanne — through Roger Fry, which was more realistically orientated. A second influence was the Euston Road School which set out to express a rather mystical and mathematical structure, including surface pimples and craters. Both these schools of drawing, which had an important influence in their time, devalued curvature and the generalised statement which goes with it. The emotional element in these two schools was also much cooler and often sublimated into remoteness. Realism demands clinical observation and preferably without comment. Iain could not stand a cold blooded expression in art, which is really the world of the realist. For that matter, too, he equally abhorred the cold blooded realist approach to people. In realism emotion is sublimated and a person, apple or tree is the subject of an analytical optical and intellectually objective study. The approach to form is questioning on the basis of what is the nature and meaning of the subject being viewed. It forms an important order of expression in art and naturally produces results quite different from Iain's classical poetry. The realist position is summed up in the work of Leonardo da Vinci and Gustave Courbet. Courbet said in reply to a dealer "Why do you not paint angels?" Courbet replied, "I will paint them when I can see them in the studio." There was no fun, grace or comment in the realist vision for Iain. Also in these islands we have not produced very many good realists. It would appear to be foreign to our nature.

The Nineteenth century philosopher Henri Louis Bergson in his "Essai sur les donnees immediates de la conscience" has this to say on rhythm and curves in relation to aesthetics. "The aesthetic feelings offer us a still more striking example of this progressive stepping in of new elements, which can be detected in the fundamental emotion and which seem to increase its magnitude, although in reality they do nothing more than alter its nature. Let us consider the simplest of them, the feeling of grace. At first it is only the perception of a certain ease, a certain facility in the outward movements. And as those movements are easy which prepare the way for others, we are led to find a superior ease in the movements which can be foreseen, in the present attitudes in which future attitudes are pointed out and, as it were, prefigured. If jerky movements are wanting in grace, the reason is that each of them is self-sufficient and does not announce those which are to follow. If curves are more graceful than broken lines, the reason is that, while a curved line changes its direction at every moment, every new direction is indicated in the preceding one. Thus the perception of ease in motion passes over into the pleasure of mastering the flow of time and of holding the future in the present. A third element comes in when the graceful movements submit to a rhythm and are accompanied by music. For the rhythm and measure, by allowing us to foresee to a still greater extent the movements of the dancer, make us believe that we now control them. As we guess almost the exact attitude which the dancer is going to take, he seems to obey us when he really takes it; the regularity of the rhythm establishes a kind of communication between him and us, and the periodic returns of the measure are like so many invisible threads by means of which we set in motion this imaginary puppet. Indeed, if it stops for an instant our hand in its impatience cannot refrain from making a movement, as though to push it, as though to replace it in the midst of this movement, the rhythm of which has taken complete possession of our thoughts and will. Thus a kind of physical sympathy enters into the feeling of grace."

So far in our search for the underlying aesthetic principle, which made Iain such a significant draughtsman the former considerations of rhythm and curvature concern the basic two dimensional structure and Iain was solidly committed to the third dimension. In his painting, engraving and drawing the three dimensional pictorial language had of necessity to add up when presented on a flat two dimensional plane. As soon as we begin to consider the world of solids and space from Cezanne onwards, as we must, then we run into trouble with curvature, and in Iain's case the curvature is major, generalised and emotive. Three dimensional volume he captures and defines through suggestion. All the wrong things for the period in which he lived and worked. The direct line of the development of drawing based upon curvature concepts starts with the classical Raphael, then through to Rubens and Delacroix. Such a concept is very firmly based upon the curved form of the human being and biological form. Indeed, if they were not, how then could the forms change in terms of four dimensional growth. Meninsky's drawing was also based upon these concepts, and together these two draughtsmen were, in their time forming a significant counter movement and influence through teaching, to the more dominant pressures then exerted by the Bloomsbury and Euston Road Schools. Both these Schools owed their realist concepts, cloudy or otherwise to the post-Cezanne world of form. To run contrary to this flow was to be in isolation.

From Cezanne onwards the drawing and painting of form became particularised. This is a natural consequence of the form research which made the art revolution of this century possible and inevitable. The emphasis of form was laid upon structure and space and the prevailing concept of structure from Cubism onwards was architectonic in character. In this there is little room for form concepts based upon curvature. Curvature was sublimated and severely treated in a diffuse manner. The switch here is that an architectonic structure is a generalised instrument, which Iain would not accept, his curvature had to carry the generalised statement. Once Iain had made up his mind, no influence however strong and no concept however virulent would cause him to turn a hair. On the Cezanne and Cubist influence he made his views known in his usual cheeky manner when writing for students of drawing. "I have found that the student, once he has discovered the existence of planes, is apt to be carried away by his enthusiasm and may think that by cutting up his forms into planes he is giving some mysteriously significant quality to an otherwise quite ordinary drawing. This is not always confined to students. In the years just after the war there was a spate of pictures of square apples, cubic countrysides and rhombic nudes, by young painters a little uncertain whether they were following Cezanne or bowdlerising Cubism. Now, it is an excellent exercise for the student to carve his drawing into planes, but he need not perform his exercises in public. Planes do not make a Picasso. They are, I repeat, merely part of the draughtsman's technical equipment, and will no more make him a great artist than the possession of a silverpoint will make him an Old Master." This statement was Iain's reply to Bloomsbury and the Euston Road Schools. Iain's influence at that time was well balanced by his own School the Grosvenor School of Art.

In this way Iain has rejected the architectonic structural concepts of these two schools of drawing which bridge the gap between the second and third dimensions, and it is the better for him to make this important jump in his own words. "The two dimensional linear curvature and rhythms are not outlines. They might be described as 'lines of force', for they are symbols used to express the two dimensional swing and movement of solid forms, and to give life and unity to drawing. It is obvious that the human form has volume and solidity, and that in drawing the figure we must consider the third dimension, depth. What may be by no means obvious is that volume and depth have an aesthetic meaning for the creative artist. There is no aesthetic virtue in solidity for the sake of solidity, and the third dimension is used to increase the rhythmical movement of form. The forms are analysed and then synthetized into solid symbols to create a further life, a rhythmical movement in depth.

It takes considerably more than angular or curved forms to make a Picasso or a Rubens. Planes, solidity, bulk, and volume, all these have no more pictorial significance than the pencil or charcoal. Their significance lies in their use as a means of expression. What the draughtsman expresses by their means is what matters." The drawings illustrated in this book certainly bears out this statement.

The increase of the rhythmical movement of form is the function of counterpoint. And it is counterpoint and the extension of rhythm which is Iain's answer to all the critics of curvature. From this point of view his critics might well read Bergson again. In art generally curvature is feared as an emotional vehicle moving headlong into excess. The background for this fear stems from the artist's solid devaluation of Art Nouveau. One of the weakest form aesthetics ever to enter the field of art and one of the worst demonstrations of emotional excesses dissipating form into mere decoration. The fact that even engineers fell in love with it and built it into all our railway stations could not prolong its short but very active life.

Iain finally completes his three dimensional concept of form in two statements he published on Rubens. He considered Rubens to be one of the greatest artists who ever lived. A choice between, Rubens, Rembrandt, Michaelangelo, Leonardo da Vinci, El Greco or Raphael is a good one, a policy statement, and a final choice will depend very much upon whether the one making the choice is classically, romantically or realistically inclined. Iain's concept and Rubens does add up, but in making this choice he switches back in time and cuts across Cezanne altogether. However the authority of Rubens is sound, and Iain is a Scotsman who is determined to go his own way.

In 1959 in his book, "Figure Drawing" he has this to say on Rubens. "Some consider that Rubens was a greater draughtsman and Michaelangelo although perhaps not so great a painter of individual figures. This however makes him all the more interesting as a painter, for his forms are usually not those of separate figures. They fuse and flow one into the other as they swing diagonally across the canvas.

The drawing is composed of three dimensional forms, but the movement of the design is entirely two dimensional, revealing his Baroque urge to create a movement of mass up and through his picture. This was of greater moment to him than any literary or other content. His Biblical subjects have none of the spirituality of the early Italians, nor have they the solemnity and awe of Rembrandt's religious paintings; but they have a vitality and a passionate joy in the surge and flow of human form, which mark him as a great master." Ten years later his views on Rubens are unchanged. "Rubens form flows more swiftly across the canvas than those of the earlier painters.... They are hurled triumphantly along so that the one flows into another as the whole throng sweeps throught the picture. He had none of the austerity of the Byzantines.... For all his earthiness he was a very great artist."

In this and the preceding quotation Iain is laying much stress on complexity and unity. In his work these two elements are fused. Bernard Meninsky had this to say regarding complexity and unity. "The mind delights in unity, but it would be unwise to confuse the term 'unity' with the more commonly used 'simplification'. Unity can only be realised through an intense study of a given form, relating the parts to the whole by virtue of unremitting search and discovery, whilst 'simplification' is only too often an arbitrary way of reducing a given form to a schematized simplicity for the sake of an obvious and often sterile decorative end. Unity is in fact not incompatible with complexity, and very often is all the more striking when it grows out of it."

There is another way of approaching the qualities of unity, simplicity, complexity and order which Iain and Bernard Meninsky were writing about. These qualities are essential to all great works of art and there is a need for measure and assessment of these qualities in fields other than art. There are two ends to this concept of value, one the producer end and the other the consumer end of the scale. For instance it is necessary for the psychologist to make a degree of measure when he is considering the relationship between Mr. Everyman and the aesthetic appreciation and the place of a work of art in the scheme of things. There are also many objects which have an aesthetic character and values, but are in no way classed as works of art. Two different types of article come to mind in this context, the aircraft and the pot. The first object is mechanical and has to perform a function, whereas the second has to perform a function but need not be mechanical in production. Both forms can be graceful, and it would not be unreasonable to refer to them as works of art, which they are not and in such reference we would only be adding a form of praise. This is of course paying homage to mechanical complexity and the simplicity of two graceful orders of form. The production methods and the mechanical nature of both does allow for any number being made to the same specification. The differences here in maximum complexity is that a work of art must be a unique, unrepeatable maximum of complexity and order.

Fechner, the Nineteenth century psychologist and psycho-physicist devised an aesthetic principle by which the values of a work of art could be approximately expressed, to have meaning for use in fields of study other than in art. He quite rightly concluded that people generally were very quickly bored by a single area of colour on a two dimensional, rectangular colour chip, regardless of the fact that the rectangle was based upon the Golden Sector, a dynamic proportion. The form so described is the most simple. He also established that interest and response increased as the colours multiplied and shapes grew in complexity. Fechner then realised that the greatest interest and response by the largest number and widest variety of people over the longest period of time was firmly held by the acknowledged great works of art. A work of art, whether in architecture or art, represents a maximum of complexity, which is always characterised by a unity or order. Most people would agree that these qualities are essential for a work of art to be designated as such. From this sequence Fechner formulated his principle $M = \dfrac{O}{C}$. His M represents aesthetic Measure and value assessment. C is Complexity required for perceptual effort and O is Order, unity, harmony or symmetry, which is the quality the subject must have if it is to be classified as aesthetic. Birkhoff is the mathematician who extended the work and produced a large count in its support. The Fechner-Birkoff principle has been the subject of much critical analysis and testing by change and time, but it still has much real value.

The Raphael Cartoons so well loved by many people of many generations stand for one of the highest achievements in drawing and colour. Such a scale alone is super-human. The whole is composed for a building, and each separate cartoon a unique composition within the whole and every figure, so noble, powerful, graceful and eloquent is a smaller unit of the whole, and these proportions and rhythms extend into the parts of heads, hands and feet. Yet these most masculine of men, the Apostles, have never been seen to live, and in real life several of the Apostles had very mean physical characteristics, and all of them were much less than Raphael has depicted them. Yet these cartoons are some of the worlds greatest poetry. Does the man in the street like these Apostles because he would wish all men to be of such physical stature?

Sir Joshua Reynolds in the thirteenth discourse which he delivered to the students at the Royal Academy in 1786, also defined the aesthetic measure of complexity and unity from which poetry can take flight. "Poetry addresses itself to the same faculties and the same dispositions as painting, though by different means. The object of both is to accommodate itself to all the natural propensities and inclinations of the mind. The very existence of poetry depends on the licence it assumes of deviating from actual nature, in order to gratify natural propensities by other means, which are found by experience full as capable of affording such gratification. It sets out with a language in the highest degree artificial, a construction of measured words, such as never is or ever was used by man.... When this artificial mode has been established as the vehicle of sentiment, there is another principle in the human mind, to which the work must be referred, which still renders it more artificial, carries it still from common nature, and deviates only to render it more perfect. That principle is the sense of congruity, coherence, and consistency, which is a real existing principle in man; and it must be gratified. Therefore, having once adopted a style and a measure not found in common discourse, it is required that the sentiments also should be in the same proportion elevated above common nature, from the necessity of there being an agreement of the parts among themselves, that one uniform whole may be produced."

Classical art is then completely artificial and therefore very abstract and pure in concept. It is the work arising from a mind which is unable to accept the Romantic or Realistic standpoint. The world of form is reconstructed or modified to give expression to a world reformed and totally organised in the concept and mode of the artist. Iain's relationship to the concept of pure abstraction is an important consideration and critical to the time in which he lived. On this issue the Twentieth century world of form was to be completely split asunder.

Very many times Iain has said, "I cannot accept pure abstraction, which is completely divorced from visual reality in my work." But he studied pure abstraction and he enjoyed good works arising in this field. He produced some completely abstract works in painting, but in engraving no single work exists. He also discussed this concept with his friends to great depths and he usually concluded the discussion with the statement, "I like people too much." He would also say, "I have nothing vital to say in form, divorced from visual reality." He was always absolutely honest. In painting he was able to turn out a highly professional and sensitive abstract work, and leave it at that. When the waters divided he knew exactly where he stood. The waters did divide.

In this century in this country, possibly the most significant events which influenced artists' lives one way or the other were the two Post Impressionist Exhibitions staged by Roger Fry at the Old Grafton Galleries in 1910 and 1911. The impact of these events depended very much upon the age group of artists at the time. Iain was at the critical formative age of 20 to 21 years. He was then free from a long production line of work trailing behind him and he was yet to make his mark in art. The older generation of artist was in a much greater dilemma of having to choose sides or redirections in face of a longer period of production. The impact of the Post Impressionists Exhibitions were however decisive and a point of no return had been made. An aesthetic fence had been erected clearly dividing artists into one side or another and many chose the certain failure of sitting on the fence. A complete change was to take place in all the arts concerned with form and space and this was to change throughout the whole world. But at that time the future could not be foreseen and there was no previous experience available to help artists to decide which turning to take. The more sensitive and creative artists did however know deep down in the conscious minds that change was inevitable, and the time was ripe, but which way and where was it to lead was quite another matter, this required imagination, courage, vision and self confidence.

Public reaction was very sharp and they threatened to burn the Grafton Gallery down and police had to be stationed there to keep law and order. The critical climate at the time is well illustrated in the exhibition report by Robert Ross, in the Morning Post, November 7, 1910. The pictures were by Cezanne, Gauguin, Van Gogh, Henri Matisse, Picasso, etc. "A date more favourable than the fifth of November for revealing the existence of a widespread plot to destroy the whole fabric of European painting, could hardly have been chosen.... There is no doubt whatever that the vast majority of the pictures.... will be greeted by the public with a.... damning and.... permanent ridicule. When the first shock of merriment has been experienced, there must follow, too, a certain feeling of sadness that distinguished critics, whose profound knowledge and connoisseurship are beyond question, should be found to welcome pretension and imposture.... If the movement is spreading.... it should be treated like the rat plague in Suffolk. The source of the infection (e.g. the pictures) ought to be destroyed."Fifty years later the National Gallery was glad to pay £33,000 for a Cezanne, which at the time of the exhibition could have been purchased for approximately £75. Deduct from this princely sum of £75 the $33\frac{1}{3}$% dealers commission, the cost of framing and publicity and Cezanne's cost of materials the residue could hardly be considered as a serious motive for producing such works. Now Cezannes have been sold for one quarter of a million pounds. In these matters we seem never to show signs of improvement.

Looking back from our time and experienced position it is perhaps even funnier to read W.B. Richmond following the exhibition in the Morning Post on November 16, 1910. (The works) "showed intellectual, emotional, and technical degeneracy; wilful anarchy and notoriety-hunting, which, were it not transparent, might be compared with criminality.

Poor Manet! It is scarcely fair to attribute the parentage of this rotten egotism to him, a disagreeable artist, a brutal painter, yet a man of genius... Cezanne might well be the father of the Post-Impressionists. Mr. Ross thinks he might have become an artist. I differ. Cezanne mistook his vocation. He should have been a butcher.... One will try and forget the joyless and melancholy exhibition.... It was a relief to breathe the petroleum-ladened air of Bond Street; even the chill of a November afternoon became invigorating as a kind of message of health after the suffocating tomb containing scarcely even the ashes of intelligence. For a moment there came even a fierce feeling of terror lest the youth of England, promising fellows, might be contaminated here....

It would be nauseating to myself and your readers to dwell on details. It would be almost as unpleasant to read as to see. There is no fear for permanent mischief, I hope. The thing is too bad for that. There is no regeneration for deluded egoists. They are morally lost in the inferno where Dante places the unfaithful to God....

I hope the press will teem with resentment against the insults offered to the noble arts of design, sculpture and painting, and insult, also, to the taste of the English people.... This innovation of depressing rubbish, is, thank heaven, new to our island of sensible, and in their own fashion, poetic people."

Against this background Iain had little trouble in making up his own mind where he stood as an artist. Together we had a lot of fun reading these reviews. There is however something sad in viewing this picture of sixty years ago. Revolt was so widespread, and so much lucid talent was lost through confusion and blindness, both to art and in writing. In these exhibitions Roger Fry had introduced the early stages of Cubism to London. Roger Fry at this time was set on a course of high critical achievement. One ism was to follow another in quick succession and each one stage by stage succeeded in a total illumination of the three dimensional representational image.

In Paris at this time Guillaume Apollinaire, the influential critic and poet was saying in his "Les Peintres Cubistes", which appeared serially in the early twenties in the American Magazine, "Little Review" (edited by Jane Heap and Margaret Anderson), "The secret aim of the young painters of the extremist schools is to produce pure painting. Theirs is an entirely new plastic art. It is still in its beginnings, and is not yet as abstract as it would like to be. Most of the new painters depend a good deal on mathematics, without knowing it; but they have not yet abandoned nature, which they still question patiently, hoping to learn the right answers to the questions raised by life." He then continues, "The new artists have been violently attacked for their preoccupation with geometry. Yet geometrical figures are the essence of drawing. Geometry, the science of space, its dimension and relations, has always determined the norms and rules of painting."

The whole orientation of the School of Paris, led by Picasso, Braque, Mattise, Roualt, Leger, Juan Gris, Zadkin and Laurens and others were pursuing a very clear direction of abstraction, regardless of the birth of numerous isms, which followed in the wake of the most important one Cubism. Later the Parisian artists were to form an immovable block, which was to arise from the birth of the German Bauhaus. Both concepts being irreconcilable one with the other. The Bauhaus was realist in concept and character and the French concept of form was classical and still is very firmly based upon visual reality and the retention of the representational image. Abstract form concepts arising from the School of Paris start with an object, which can be an orange or human figure and to express the essence of the form, the form must be abstracted through until the essence is established, through the process of reduction. As always with this concept, abstraction is always a matter of degree, and this degree can proceed until abstraction is virtually complete, but the source of inspiration is always discernible in the end product.

The concept of abstraction from the School of Paris had a completeness as far as painting and sculpture was concerned, but its inherent weakness lay in its ability to properly embrace architecture. They did of course have Le Corbusier, the architect within their ranks working as a cubist painter and designer, and he also absorbed cubism into his personal style, but architecturally his style was too personal to give rise to a school producing new architecture. He had a lot of followers who were however stylistically influenced and thereby unable to contribute new form experience to architecture. The same thing applies to all followers, and no one has had more than Picasso and the result is the same.

A further watershed of form was to arrive with the development of the Bauhaus in Weimar from 1919 to 1925 and at Dessau from 1925 to 1932. The Bauhaus was disbanded by Hitler, as being degenerate and anti-state. It was reformed again as the New Bauhaus in Chicago in 1937-1938, and it was later known as the School of Design Chicago from 1939-1944 and from this progression of moves and changes followed the Institute of Design. No school of form and of teaching in the Twentieth century has had such a fundamental influence on world art and design as has the Bauhaus. The Bauhaus was not an institution, but an idea which was formulated by the architect Walter Gropius. He set out to bring together all creative fields into one whole and to synthesise all the disciplines of art, which included a new architecture, sculpture, painting, design and the crafts. The idea was conceived as a great structure in which there would be no distinction between monumental and decorative art. Form research in all the fields of architecture, the plastic arts and the crafts was aimed at finding and developing the forms most suitable for the machine age, the essential forms required for life in the Twentieth century and above all to use the machine age to produce forms both functional and beautiful in themselves, to be used and enjoyed by the great wide public. If these design principles were applied to the mass production machinery, then art and design could really go across to the public and not be confined to those with a high income. The Bauhaus succeeded where the English craft movement failed. Ruskin and William Morris turned their vision and crafts backward, in opposition to the machine, to the point of their wishing to destroy the machine. Instead of as at the Bauhaus, mastering the machine and designing for it. The extent of the success of this operation is all well known.

Possibly the most incredible and certainly the most unexplainable aspect of Gropius's genius and idea was the staff he managed to gather around him, to fire the idea and to provide the dynamism, which turned the idea into a reality and change the whole world of form and the forming process in all the arts and crafts. A more cosmopolitan staff would be a rare find. They included Germans, Americans, Hungarians, Russians, Austrians and Swiss. The French and the English were notably absent. A short list of staff names at the Bauhaus will suffice as an illustration. Working with Gropius the architect we find Albers, Arndt, Bayer, Breuer, Feininger, Hilberseimer, Itten, Kandinsky, Klee, Marcks, Meyer, Moholy Nagy, Muche, Schlemmer, Schmidt, and later the very influential architect Mies v.d. Rohe. The school operated as a workshop, with no teachers or pupils, but masters, journeymen and apprentices.

Our chief concern is however the fundamental changes brought about in drawing and teaching by the researches of Klee and Kandinsky during their Bauhaus period. Paul Klee atomised and took apart the whole means of an artist's method of expression. This proved to be the final blow, and complete irradication of the representational image from pictorial art. From Klee everything starts from a dot or point. It is what is done from there onwards that matters. Two dots or points will imply a line. A line is a pure abstraction and must therefore remain pure and not be made to represent anything out of its true context, such as twisting its illusory way round an image of a three dimensional form. Two lines meeting introduces a new element, the angle which implies direction. And a plane arises as a number of lines lying parallel to each other. Klee then **develops** line through to the plane and its ultimate relationship to tone and colour and thereby completes a reconstruction of three dimensional form. He then arrives with all the elements of form, free and pure in their own right. The subject matter of the work was to evolve at the end of the process, rather than as previously at the very beginning. This analytical realist approach to art establishes for the first time the autonomy of a pure abstract art. An art which need have no subject matter. It was an art comprising of pure form. Virtually as pure as music. When Klee and the Bauhaus began to be seen, felt and discussed in this country, it was the straw, which was to virtually break the camel's back. Once again the reactions were violent and heated. Another fence had been erected to divide artists into one camp or another, plus the percentage who choose to wither away by sitting on the fence. Even Paris would not admit that anything fundamental to art could happen outside of Paris and Bauhausian art and design was resisted for a very long time. It was of course Germanic in origin and Teutonic in discipline. Also it was too close to science and technology. It was a purely realist manifestation and this is an anathema to the French temperament. But one more important fact remains the concept was open ended and was about life itself rather than what art was, or should be.

A diamond is to many people many things. To a woman it is often referred to as her best friend. A financier will see only size, weight and its market value. An industrialist would view it as a machine tool which would cut the hardest metals. A jeweller would polish it to give the maximum light reflection, but he need not fully appreciate the light mechanics of the form. A photographer would only be equipped to record a part of the image and have to be satisfied with a very superficial impression. An illustrator would endeavour to imitate its superficial appearance. The representational artist would view the form as a major problem in the exercise of painting white light and creating an optical deception through the reflected light and colour surrounding the diamond, but which is not part of it. To the realist or Bauhausian painter, however the diamond would be a structure starting with the constituent wavelengths that comprise white light and the angles of reflection, refraction and diffusion, which occur immediately light strikes a transmitting material surface. The facets are arranged as a geometric sequence around the form, which is designed to create a multiplicity of angles of reflection and refraction to pass the light beam to and fro inside the form. The arrangements of the form are then responsible for the defracted beams displaying the vibrating hues of many wavelengths. The totally internally reflected light beams then distinguish between the natural and the artificial diamond. A Bauhausian realist must start with the source of the structure and progress as far as he can and he may well not arrive at a complete diamond. In significance however the light structure comprising the diamond is the greater reality to stimulate the imagination. Inside the diamond is a world as beautiful and complex, although unseen as is the world of light surrounding it. The world surrounding the transmitting diamond is then a continuation by reflection. Such continuity of form and structure does lead us into the continuum, which is the world of four dimensional form. A further illustration of this form world is more simply demonstrated by the man walking from point A to B and in the process is blowing up a balloon. Explain what happens to the balloon. The balloon expands simultaneously in every dimension. It could not effect this change without the time and space in which to expand. The man walking from point A to B is kinetic time and no real consequence, as in the process there is virtually no change in his form. This world of form and structure will give us a better understanding of the strange and disturbing set of Storm drawings which appeared during the last five years of Leonardo da Vinci's life. As with the diamond, so with the non-visible storm in the air, Leonardo drew and exposed the structure of storms and reflected this structure into the surrounding background, the forms of which were actually being moulded by the storm structure. The structure was thereby in a continuum, just as in the transparent diamond and the reflecting forms surrounding it. These concepts of form have common ground and Klee did say in his Jenna lectures that he set out, not to render the visible, but to render visible. This is precisely what Leonardo did in those last, great and eventful five years. Today of course we understand the diamond, the better through science. Once a fact is known the realist cannot ignore it. Neither for that matter could a realist of today come to the same conclusions as for instance Courbet.

Figure 23 —   *Winter Landscape 1927*

Figure 24 — *Le Quai de Isle. Annecy 1929*

Figure 25 —   *The Waterfront. Calvi Corsica. 1930*

Figure 26 — *Corsican Landscape. 1931*

Figure 27 — *Majorcan Village. 1932*

Figure 28 – *Southern Landscape. 1933*

Figure 29 — *Fishermen. Portofino. 1936*

Figure 30 — *Two Fat Ladies, Portofino. 1936*

Figure 31 — *Drying Sails. Lake Garda 1938*

Figure 32 – *Fishermen, Battersea Park. 1948*

Figure 33 – *Water Lilies. 1960*

Figure 34 — *Ronda Bridge. Spain 1961*

5 - The composer

The composing process is subject to a continual rise and fall of imagination and energy, which is the fuel exciting the creative dynamo. Iain's dynamo was highly charged throughout his life, in fact, right to the end, it never flagged.

Iain was a dynamic and powerful composer and his conception was classical in approach and orientated on pictorial structure. The pictorial structure was completely worked out from individual drawings and studies, through to the final work. Many of his engravings were followed by paintings. He used to say that he was able to work the painting tones out better in an engraving. We can see him at work in the engraving "The Brave Bull" 1951, *Fig. 11* and *Fig. g,* which is an outstanding example of classical composition and form. All the pictorial elements are directed towards a concentrated centre. *Fig.g* illustrates the underlying structure, which is based upon a system of triangulation, to establish the major aesthetic movements of thrust from the right and counter thrust from the left. The total compositional form is an all embracing triangle, which is bisected by the central spear to give a secondary pair of triangles within the large one. This structure brings the bull and horse well into the play in the centre and the bull fighters are brought in around the core or centre to complete the main triangular form. The double triangle giving the sharp angular form, diamond in character, was used on many of Goya's compositions in the "La Tauromaquia" series of etchings. Iain's angles are however determined by and drawn from the subject and not any superimposed theoretical geometry. If these angles had been exactly 90° the work would have been sterile instead of dynamic.

We can follow the development of his thinking as a composer through his writing on the subject. On classical theory he has this to say, "The abstract qualities, which the classical draughtsman endeavours to express are not based on any ordinary canons of beauty such as ideal proportions or symmetry of the human form. Neither are they connected with any human emotion felt towards the model nor by the model. They are based on the classical theory which we find first propounded by Plato, that certain arrangements of curved and angular shapes, and of solid and linear forms, will give pleasure to the eye, and that the pleasure experienced in contemplating these designs cannot be accounted for by associating them with the visual appearances of natural forms. We may describe their significance as being purely pictorial and quite unconnected with any representational or descriptive content.

If we analyse our sensations very carefully, we shall find in most cases that we have unconsciously responded to some dynamic quality in a group of forms of this nature. This quality of vitality may be caused by any or all of the following:— harmonies, juxtapositions of curves with angular or straight lines, or variations of size, colour, tone or texture.

The pleasure which the artist experiences in drawing from the figure comes first from the perceptual discovery of these abstract qualities; secondly, from their emotive conception in his mind; and thirdly, from arranging his symbols in an ordered design which will exteriorise his conception and make visible his sensations."

This is a very clear statement on what he means by the term classical form. Canons of beauty based upon ideal proportions or symmetry are really laws rather than concepts and may suit one period of time but have no relevance for another period. Ideal proportions are of much greater interest in mathematics, than when used as a dominant law in the creation of form. The effect can be very stultifying and repressive. At the same time all art concepts, excepting the romantic are the better for having maths as their spring board or underlying motivation. But if maths, which can in the hands of an artist quickly degenerate into a formula, are then used as a law in the forming process, then the important possibility of change has virtually been ruled out. The mathematician however would effect and control change through the development of maths, but the artist very rarely achieves this. The need for aesthetic change will in most cases cause him to break with maths and thereby become mathematically illogical. Iain then extends this theme in his statement on composition and pictorial emotion, which is illuminating and gives a very clear insight into this aspect of his art and thinking. "Only by deliberate selection and emphasis can the artist hope to convey something of the emotive effect upon his senses of the discovery that permeating everything about him even the commonest objects and the dullest surroundings in this life, beauty, dynamic significance or whatever other name one cares to give it. The stronger his reaction the more forceful will he strive to recreate it in his picture. It is axiomatic that only by over-statement can the artist avoid under-statement, and by exaggeration speak the truth.

In drawing, the emotive expression of the forms is of greater importance than their factual description. But the artist must never be swept off his feet by uncontrolled emotion-alism. He must be capable of analysing his sensations before he can attempt to synthesize even then, although he may not always be conscious of doing so. It will make him realise that without a preconceived design he cannot hope to give his work any emotional significance. His sensations may be most profound and important aesthetically, but without a language in which to communicate them, he will find himself with nothing to say. In forming this conception he need not see the finished picture in his mind. Very few artists can do so, and few attempt to do so at this stage; but he must be able to see what we may call the skeleton of the design and he must know how to build upon that.

The artist's reaction and his conception will probably take place intuitively and perhaps simultaneously in his mind; but although he may paint without conscious effort, and "as the bird sings" as Monet used to say, he must be able to bring these into consciousness if neces-sary. No picture grows by chance, and although the "Hit-or-miss" artist may bring off some lucky flukes, he is lost if his luck does not hold.

It goes without saying that imaginative composition does not mean a picture in which the artist has attempted either to alter nature or to paint something he has never seen. To the intelligent spectator it means a picture which is charged with emotional significance, and which evokes those emotions because of the pictorial, and not the descriptive, meaning of its symbols. Its design should communicate these sensations to us even before we realise what is its subject matter.

When we survey the history of pictorial expression we find that it has been one of continued striving to create fresh life. Every time that a new way of doing this has been discovered, there has been a spurt forward."

The engraving "Ronda Bridge, Spain" 1961 *Fig.34* is a composition produced at the height of his maturity, which is architectural in character. It is emotive, unusually simple, and a large wedge of black set in and surrounded by a changing world of light, sensitive textures. Yet each texture is evocative of its source, grass, sand, rocks, vegetation, trees and clouds. Each rendered in terms of the tool used and only simulating such things as grass, rocks or sky. The massive proportions of the bridge and its simple contrasting treatment gives to the composition a scale, which is big and appears larger than the actual physical dimensions of 20.3 x 25.4 centimeters. Such sensitivity can only arise firstly from the realisation of sheer strength. This engraving gives a clear indication as to what comprises aesthetic emotion. Some of the cutting in the two vertical planes of the ravine are so fine, that even the camera is unable to record the extremely fine black and white spacing. Because of the closeness of the engraving we exper-ience the shimmering silvery grey in the bottom left hand side of the vertical plane of the ravine. Iain often said that, "Watered down aesthetics were a very bad companion for an artist." It is not for nothing that the English artist has to meet the Continental charge, that, the English so often fail to drive their aesthetic home.

Iain's statements on composition makes his vision and the relationship to the two dom-inant Schools of abstraction, the School of Paris and the Bauhaus, very clear. He held firmly and intelligently to the French concept of applying abstraction to visual reality with a view to reducing the form to its essentials. All his drawings and engraving demonstrate the unwavering point of view. As with most Scottish artists, Iain felt himself stylistically and emotionally more akin to the French than the English character. From the point of view of his own work, but not in others, he flatly refused the realist concept of Bauhausian form. However no Contin-ental in art will be able to say that he failed to push his aesthetic of form home, good, clean and sharp. His logic of form and its development and excitment in living is also close to the

French temperament. On several occasions these qualities came under attack in the press. The English flavour calls for sublimation of emotion.

There are many terms used by artists, to describe activities and qualities, where in numerous other disciplines and studies different terms have been adopted as standard. Iain uses the word "tone" which in science and industry is represented by the term "value". In his statement Iain uses the word "pictorial" in relation to emotion in preference to the generally used critical term "aesthetic" and he gives us a very clear picture of the relationships and values he placed on the "aesthetic" or "pictorial" emotion. He also describes very clearly his conception of classical structure. Iain needed the stability of classical form, possibly to counterpoint the cut, thrust and flux of life as he found it. He often said, "You will only find peace, way up with the angels." It was classical form and its reconstruction concepts which gave him peace and the constant values he sought so much, in himself and other people. These passages also give a very clear indication of his understanding of the work of Rubens. A Rubens composition does work in just this way. His sweeping and swiftly moving compositions are articulated upon a two dimensionally conceived structure, but the forms and space surrounding the figures are rendered three dimensionally. Iain's published statements are always well supported in his work.

Figure 35 — *Illustration from Tam O' Shanter. 1934*

"Drying Sails, Lake Garda" 1938, *Fig.31* is Iain's most famous composition. The composition is masterly and subtle and the engraving is a phenomenal technical achievement. It is also a brilliant exercise in the distribution of counter rhythms beautifully equated to form the basis for the aesthetic emotion. The composition gives Iain's perfect answer to the Rubens principle of swinging a complete and complex three dimensional world across the canvas on a two dimensional structure.

Single lines in art can also become famous in their own right. They do however have to be something very special, like Giotto's O, or the story told by Pliny about Apelles and Protogenes. "Apelles landed, one day, on the Isle of Rhodes, and went to see the work of Protogenes, who lived there. Protogenes was not in the studio when Apelles arrived. An old woman was there, looking after a large canvas which the painter had prepared. Instead of leaving his name, Apelles drew on the canvas a line so subtle that nothing better could be conceived.

Returning, Protogenes saw the line, recognised the hand of Apelles, and drew on the latter's line another line of another colour, one even more subtle, so that it seemed as if there were three lines.

Apelles came back the next day, and again did not find his man; the subtlety of the line which he drew this time cause Protogenes to despair. The sketch aroused for many years the admiration of connoisseurs, who contemplated it with as much pleasure as if it had depicted gods and goddesses, instead of almost invisible lines."

Iain's superb linear achievement is just visible as they are the two sets of three ropes securing the masts to the boat hulls. These lines, straight and in their continuous track, change from white on black to black on white without breach, slip, damage or coarseness and are perfect, fine and sensitive in their flow one in relation to the other. Where the line is black the end grained boxwood has to be carved and the line left standing, and where the lines are white the burin has cut a V shaped furrow. The superhuman aspect is of course the length, not of one but of six. Yet these lines are much more than brilliant technical achievement, they form the theme of the composition itself. The boats and sails are there for these lines and show the composition structure, the role these six lines play, its rhythms and counter rhythm articulation. Counterpoint arises from the remarkable T theme. The T joint is also a fundamental principle of architecture, with the column and lintel method for spanning space, brick meeting brick and wall meeting wall. This architectural principle works both in plan and elevation and in terms of most of the materials used. It is also a load bearing principle, and as such is dynamic. Iain's T type counter rhythms are based upon the long stem and alternating short line or lintel, which gives the composition its dramatic upward surge. The boatmen form a triangular base to direct the eye of the observer on to the six lines which Iain wanted to engrave. Also these lines had to be engraved before any further lines had to cross them, otherwise there was the great danger of the burin jumping the gap. It is very rare for six lines to have so much to say.

In this picture Iain has drawn of the relationships between the emotional and the strictly pictorial values, he is remarkably close to Clive Bell's critical aesthetic of "Significant Form", which was to play such an important role in English art as we know it today and particularly in Iain's younger and more formative years. Bell's critical concept has undoubtedly had far more influence on English art than any other aesthetic. It was first published in 1914, very soon after Roger Fry's Post Impressionist Exhibitions at the Grafton Gallery. Cubism was well advanced in Paris by this time. Clive Bell's "Significant Form" concept was also the first to be based upon the premise that the aesthetic value of form must be considered in its own right and not in any way to be influenced by subject matter considerations. This would have been an absolute anathema to Ruskin. It also began to prepare the way for and the acceptance of the later developments of pure abstract art. At that time the pure abstraction of the Bauhaus was not on the horizon as far as English art was concerned.

The influence of the abstract thinking of the time did have a strong influence on Iain's work. His dramatic qualities and mastery of the principle of counter rhythms stems from his teaching work on the human figure. To make his compositional principles clear to his students he taught aesthetics. Students want fundamental design concepts and rarely meet this quality of instruction. The shock value of the sharp counter rhythm eventually resolves itself into the architectural T principle, which we see at work so skillfully in the "Drying Sails, Lake Garda" 1938. *Fig. 31.* The Rubens principle of swinging a three-dimensional complexity, rhythmically across a canvas also becomes clearly evident.

Referring to *Figs. a, b* and *c, d, e,* he says, "If we draw three lines, horizontal, vertical and oblique (*Fig. a*), of these, the first two will appear static, although the oblique line will give a certain indication of movement; but if we curve this oblique line so that it becomes roughly about a quarter of a circle (*Fig. b*) we find that we have increased its apparent movement, largely owing to the tendency of the eye to run along a curved line. If we repeat parallel lines, we make a simple harmony. If we repeat parallel lines in an ordered sequence we create a rhythm." *Fig. c* demonstrates the main linear rhythm and the main and counter rhythms are seen in *Fig. d–Fig. e* "Lines of thighs and thorax", or the models legs meeting the body, gives us the full force of counter rhythm, Rubens, Iain and the architectural T principle. Iain describes these lines (*Fig. cde*) as "lines of force".

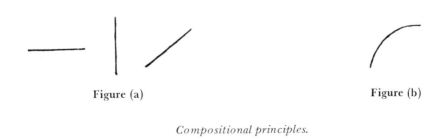

Figure (a)   Figure (b)

Compositional principles.

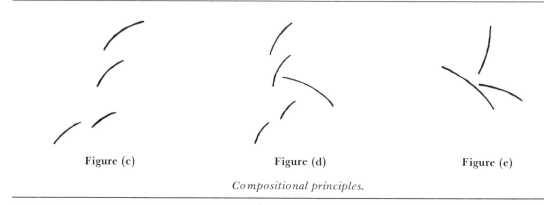

Figure (c)   **Figure (d)**   **Figure (e)**

Compositional principles.

These lines of force, the counter rhythm of the T factor, all abstract concepts can be seen to a sharp and pointed effect in *Fig.3* "Illustration from The Sculptured Garland" 1948. The solid blacks counterpoint the large white areas of the space of paper and the grey textures harmonise with the print. Unity between the type set lines is strongly established and repeated in the two hroizontal lines in the composition. The lines of force are clearly visible in *Fig. f.* Wood engraving really can crystalise this quality of expression. In the structural sense the composition itself is in excellent balance. The powerful engraving "The Waterfront, Calvi" 1930, *Fig.25* which is a study of the strong light effects, cutting the architectural scene, into sharp whites and blacks, expresses the architectural T principle rather forceably. The linear structure of the movement directing the force is illustrated. It is the bull's eye target arresting the flight of arrows. These lines of force which are very abstract make the form significant and the aesthetic emotion very real. Iain also loved the town planning aspect of architecture and he engraved several studies of compact town squares and the arrangements within them. The small enclosed square within the larger unit of the town or city is still one of our more civilised forms of town planning.

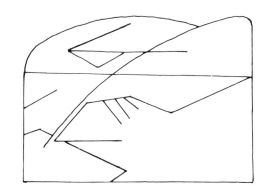

Figure (f) *Composition structure for engraving on page 14*

The stamp of an artist of real calibre, is the thorough manner in which he works out all his concepts. We can see the forceful thrusts arriving from the fundamental architectural T principle which is demonstrated in the engraving "Fishermen Portofino" 1936 and also arise as a motive in the drawing of "Two Figures", illustrated in *Figs. 29,40*. This compositional structure, which is so similar is remarkable in that the subjects of architecture and the human figure in terms of form are absolutely opposite. But then these are the terms in which the classical mind sees the world in which he finds himself.

In the drawing *Fig.43* the artist is extending the art of composing within a single form into two forms. Such a grouping gives a massive sculptural organisation of volumes, interrelated space planes and structures, both forms giving a unity of counter rhythms. His strong feeling for sculpture is evident in this drawing and the rendering of the three dimensional volumes is achieved through an extension of his brush drawing technique. This drawing is impressive for the expression of sheer gravity. His further expression of gravity can also be compared in the figure drawing *Fig.44*.

In his arrangement of the two figures in *Fig.40* we see him posing the T principle. The trunk of the model which is reclining, forms the stem and the cut off, T bar or lintel and counter rhythm is set up in the male model, cutting across the female model, and this all starts with his basic design principle, which he used for teaching purposes illustrated in *Fig.e.* The drawing is very abstract and the brush strokes express a maximum of sensitivity from the fully loaded brush to the powdered wisps of the dry brush. This is yet another demonstration of sensitivity arising from sheer strength. The lines are fast, certain and accurate, and the aesthetic emotion is expressed very sharply. It is from the breadth of composition that we are able to read the philosophy of the man.

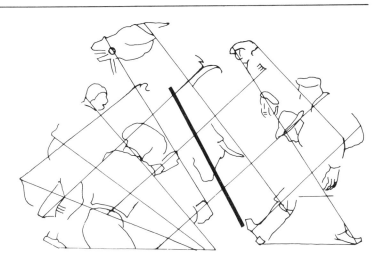

Figure (g) *Composition structure for the engraving 'The Brave Bull'*

Bell's central problem was to determine and define the aesthetic emotion. For instance Mr. Everyman can raise a lot of excitement from a confrontation with the gloriously good looking men whom Raphael uses as compositional elements in his massive "Cartoon". Also Mr. Everyman may or may not know, or be disturbed by the fact that these men of Raphael never existed as such, but who in real life were much more likely to be short, even ugly, perhaps unkempt and moulded against their natural potential by the force of circumstance, environment and their occupations. Mr. Everyman is however almost certain to miss the experience of the pure "aesthetic emotion" which arises as a supreme example of the relationships of the forms to each other and to the whole, and the vast two and three dimensional organisation which determines the position of each finger in relation to the pose, and each figure in relation to its exact position in space, and the space control in relation to the architecture. They were commissioned by Pope Leo, X, as a set of ten tapestries, destined for the Sistine Chapel in the Vatican. Three of the cartoons from the complete set no longer exist. Yet over and above all else the strongest aesthetic, or in Iain's terms "pictorial emotion" is the massive and infinite rhythms which runs through and unifies all the elements and consolidates the power and direction of the whole conception. Like a breeze animating a corn field. Very briefly Bell's concept of "Significant Form" is developed on this basis and gives him an essential quality which distinguishes a work of art from all other objects. As aesthetic values are emotionally based, then all aesthetic judgements must be and are subjective. This implies also that the measure of aesthetic enjoyment a person derives from a work of art is the measure of the effort he or she has made and brought to it. The greater the effort the greater the reward.

If a representational image has real value, it is as form and not as representation. Nothing discloses with greater clarity the difference between form and representation than life drawing. If an artist has no command of form, then in desperation he must resort to representation. The failure is then one of insensitivity which fosters the kind of desperation which gives rise to the opposite every day range of emotion. Representational elements in a work of art may or may not be harmful, but is always a vehicle for form, if not, then the representational image is irrelevant. Clive Bell emphasises the relationship of representation in his statement, "To help the spectator to appreciate our design we have introduced into the picture a representative or cognitive element. This element has nothing whatever to do with art. The recognition of a corresponding between the forms of a work of art and the familiar forms of life cannot possibly provoke aesthetic emotion. Only significant form can do that. However in a representational work of art the subject is a further means to the understanding of the formal relationships. We experience trouble when the representational aspects are primary and uppermost in concept. This does give us the concept of the illustrator. Representational elements in art must then perform two functions, firstly to be the vehicle of form expression and secondly to give information not only on the subject but on the artist and his philosophy and relationships to life in general and in Iain's particular case his intense interest in people, as individuals. Yet when we view his drawings the individual is there and sublimated to a highly abstract drawing structure."

As in most aesthetic concepts, there is a hole in Clive Bell's "Significant Form". There always will be holes or gaps in aesthetic concepts, but regardless, they are very necessary tools in the forming process, in a state of continuous change at any time or period. He undervalued meaning in a work of art. His emphasis on the non-representational elements led him to include the pot and a Persian carpet as works of art. The meaning of both these objects are pure craft, at a very high order. A work of art is a unique piece or thing and in practically every case excepting in architecture, quite useless. The pot and Persian carpet are both reproducible and are made to be used. So surely function must be dealt with and a work of art can have no such function. It is true that the form of both can be very pure and sensitively developed to excite an aesthetic emotion. But we would fail to achieve their full appreciation if we ignored the fact that they are the result of highly developed and sensitive craft, which is concerned to perform a function rather than to express a point of view. Purpose made articles can have no secure place in art aesthetics. Clive Bell devised his "Significant Form" concept at a time when he and everyone else were witnessing the progressive devaluation of the three dimensional representational image in preparation for the development of pure abstract art. He also failed in the realm of meaning, to place properly the value and character of the image. The image in some shape or form will always be an integral part of art. Form and image change continually from one period to another. In some periods the image dominates, in others it is subject to geometry, in others a mere vehicle for structure, in Surrealism the image serves theatrical purposes, in others literary ends and so on. It also undergoes fundamental changes of emphasis in the dominance of a two, three or four dimensional orientation. But meaning and image, which may ebb and flow, will be in art while there is art. The world of the image was to change again, fundamentally through the work of Paul Klee, in a manner which Clive Bell could not anticipate at the time he wrote his thesis. With Klee the image evolved formally from a basic structure and all its parts were units related to the structure and the image developed gradually as the structure was extended. Klee's image was the realisation of the whole, which came at the end of a work and not at the beginning. The image evolving at the end of the creative process or conclusion of a work was a complete reversal of previous image building process. The element of time had been built into the design process of image forming. As in architecture a main structure was determined and the extended design process evolved the secondary development of the structure and the final and small units, the bricks, related in terms of the total structure completed the work. By these means a structure and aesthetic for the expression of pure fantasy was evolved, which gave Klee the means for the development of great poetry. The complete antithesis of Klee's fantasy is the Victorian painter, William Etty's conception of fantasy. In his painting "Youth at the helm", a literary poetic concept, and not an aesthetic one, is superimposed upon a group of young healthy people, theatrically distributed in improbable positions and gleefully dancing on the decks of a romantic boat. All very skilfully rendered in the naturalistic three dimensional terms of the period. Both artists worked in terms of the human figure. One achieved aesthetic fantasy and the other failed. Another parallel to this composition comparison arises from two well known works in a different media and each directed in aim to entertaining children. Walt Disney has succeeded with children so well because his abstract image technique arises from the requirements of the cartoon filming mechanics. The form which is highly developed and very readable arises out of and in terms of the requirements of kinetics and stills. No attempt whatsoever is made to make the characters appear in naturalistic terms, thereby there is no language confusion or invitation to the child to look upon what is being seen as anything other than what it is. It is a vehicle for poetry, which children understand. Then there is the literary and illustrative world of Beatrix Potter, so well loved by so many children, when in the form of books. Also Beatrix Potter conceived the work in terms of books and the related techniques. But when this work was taken out of this context and interpreted in an adult balletic form by the Royal Ballet Company, with each member faithfully dressed and then projected to the child audience in the form of a film, it did not succeed in communication. Neither did it succeed with the adult audience, who had the experience to appreciate ballet, because obviously Beatrix Potter's world did in no way lend itself to this treatment. It represented a misdirected but heroic effort to give a grand scale conception in another art form, which was applied with English dedication and fidelity to Beatrix Potter's sensitive illustrative art which just refused to work out of context. Children were confused by form language confusion.

Figure 36 —
Illustration from the book Tam O' Shanter. 1934

In Bell's terms the form of Klee was "significant" and Etty's form when it existed was so sublimated to the literary idea as to be "insignificant". In terms of form designed for the entertainment the same criteria applies. Klee's fantasy arises from the arrangement of formal values. Walt Disney's fantasy arises in the same manner. Fantasy is real in Beatrix Potter's books, but confused and unworkable in the Beatrix Potter film. The most important difference between these comparisons is in "Meaning". It is also axiomatic that given significant form as in Klee, then the meaning of the forms image must of consequence be of great importance, towards achieving a full aesthetic appreciation. By the same token the idealistic apostle image in Raphael's Cartoons is an important extension of his form organisation and aesthetic. Bell's theory is weak on meaning. Meaning leads more directly into the inner regions of the artist's mind and indicates the reasons for much of what he is responsible for. It enables us to approach his philosophy and to ask such questions as to why he did this or that. For instance it is important in appreciation to know that the art of Picasso is destructive, and that stylistically it is an end in itself, whereas Klee is the opposite and is constructive and the beginning of a new world of form. From this aspect of meaning, we the observers immediately gain a sense of direction. Why was the meaning of Iain's form and work so rich and generous, his compositions so powerful and sensitive and his drawing so incisive and erudite? Simply stated he was like this in life, and he loved life and people as individuals who were caught up in political, economic, religious and ethnic structures that threw them one against the other and too often in a brutal bloodthirsty manner. To Iain people were exciting as individuals, but less so as instruments of Governments and creeds, much less exciting. One of Iain's very early ambitions, even before sculpture came into his mind was to be a cartoonist. He said, "You see I love people and all their idiosyncratic vagaries, and I always wanted to have fun with them." He always wished to speak with clear diction and form, he wished to attract for purposes of communication and in this matter simplicity was tantamount to success. He expressed a belief in hope and healthy living of the individual, and his composition expressed a breadth and generosity, but he had nothing to give to Government and politics. These qualities do not however speak of revolution and disruption. He had had enough of that fighting in two wars. His belief was directly anchored in the sanity of man, and his safety valve change. He abhorred the sick image, the image of no hope or joy, which has become quite frequent in present day life and art. His dislike of Surrealism was due to his dislike of private dream images made public. Secondly he disliked the formal means used by the Surrealists to project their images. His reply to the sex image was simply, that in itself it has little to commend it and in art very few succeed in making it aesthetically significant. In fact it takes a big artist to really justify the subject. His approach to other people and equally so in his art, was the message of live and let live. But most important of all, to give life to everything one does and this needs conviction. Indeed with such meaning why take up engraving at all? Its restrictions were legion and accompanied by no likelihood of ever being able to make a living from it. Iain's comments on this are expressed in his book on wood engraving and he states, "Wood engraving had been under a cloud since the "nineties", and had been looked upon as a rather old-fashioned method of reproducing drawings, and not as a form of artistic self-expression. Its very severity as a medium, however, gives it more scope for formal design; and this quality, alone with its unexploited possibilities and very definite limitations, made it all the more attractive to those artists who were affected by the contemporary trend towards clarity and simplicity of statement, more clean-cut and precise draughtsmanship, and greater insistance on design." He continues, "Again, many artists found that etching, with its unlimited capacity for sketchiness and imative impressionism, was almost too facile a process. Feeling the need for a less tractable medium and for a greater formality of expression, they either adopted a tighter and more deliberate style of drawing with the etching needle or started using the engraving tool, as the limitation imposed by the use of the graver, whether on metal or wood, make sketchy drawing and vague impressionism impossible. Every line has to be considered and has to be stated clearly and definitely so that it will take its place as part of the design.

It may sound paradoxical, but the more limitation an artist imposes upon himself by reason of an intractable medium, and the more he observes these limitations, the greater degree of freedom will he discover. By expressing himself in terms of the medium he leaves himself free to simplify his forms, and to choose symbols which will explain these forms; symbols which will be beautiful in themselves in their arrangements of form and pattern, and which will bring out the inherent beauty of that medium. To force the medium by concentrating on the mere copying and representation of appearances is more likely to rob it of its own peculiar charm and to destroy its aesthetic qualities.

Here, in wood engraving, was a medium which offered an entirely new field. As a craft its advantages were many and obvious. The materials were inexpensive and simple compared to those required for working on metal. There was not the messiness of etching nor its elaborate array of bottles of acids and other chemicals, its baths, its heaters, and its hundred and one requirements. No damping of paper and stretching of prints, and, what was more, there was no need for a press when an old spoon from the kitchen could give all the necessary pressure for a proof of one's block. Again, one was so much more mobile. The worker on metal was tied to his bench, his heater, and his press, but the wood engraver could put his block and a few tools in his pocket and go anywhere he liked." He needed this discipline to become more articulate and this was the simplicity he was seeking.

In this passage we have several clues as to why he took up this austere medium, when he was already well practised in the more fluent mediums of etching, copper engraving, lino-cutting and lithography. All these mediums can be described as fluid and expansive, and with very few limitations. Taking to these mediums is like swimming in water, all the freedom in the world is yours if you can swim, but like freedom is useless unless the right kind of swimming is

Figure 37 —
Illustration from Tam O'Shanter, 1934

developed. Just to swim around is fun for a time and freedom becomes an illusion. At all times the intellect must continually keep the available talent taut, yet balanced, if significant work is to be produced. Iain was confronted with a situation where plenty of talent and skill was always available. If then he was to realise his full potential, he had to have hard intellectual nuts to crack, and tough disciplines with which to sharpen his talent and by these means to keep it fully stretched. A five barred gate may offer a challenge too great to jump, when you have freedom and time in front of you, but place a crusty bull close behind and no question will be raised as to whether or not you will jump, but having jumped, the world becomes quite different from there onwards. A restricted medium offers the bull and gate choice. There is no sitting on the gate. This kind of decision is typical of Iain's simplicity and directness. Once he had become the wood engraver he never returned to his earlier mediums. In this respect he never vacilated. Having made the jump he stayed to fully exploit the limitations. His drawing has this tough, incisive, design discipline built into it. He also too wanted to be a sculptor but his war wounds prevented this. The engraved line did however give him the sculptural linear qualities which he valued highly. Had he been a sculptor, would he have become a stone carving sculptor? This would have been highly probable. His drawing and success in engraving suggests that he may well have done so, in much the same way as Eric Gill. With Gill the engraver moved naturally into stone sculpture, which offers the greatest challenge of all the forms of sculptural expression through the sheer toughness of the stone.

Figure 38 – *Single figure foreshortened – Jane*

Figure 39 — *Jane seated*

Figure 40 — *Triangular formation*

Figure 41 — *Star gazer — Janet*

Figure 42 — *Janet contemplating*

Figure 43 — *sculptural group*

Figure 44 — *Study of a male back*

Figure 45 — *Jane — back view*

Figure 46 — *Janet — alert*

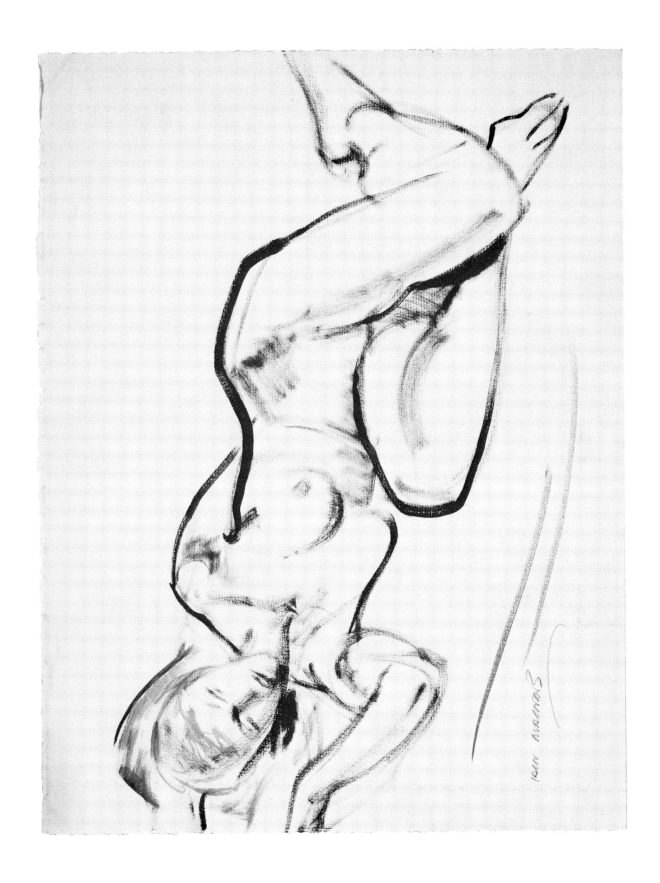

Figure 47 — *Janet — reclining*

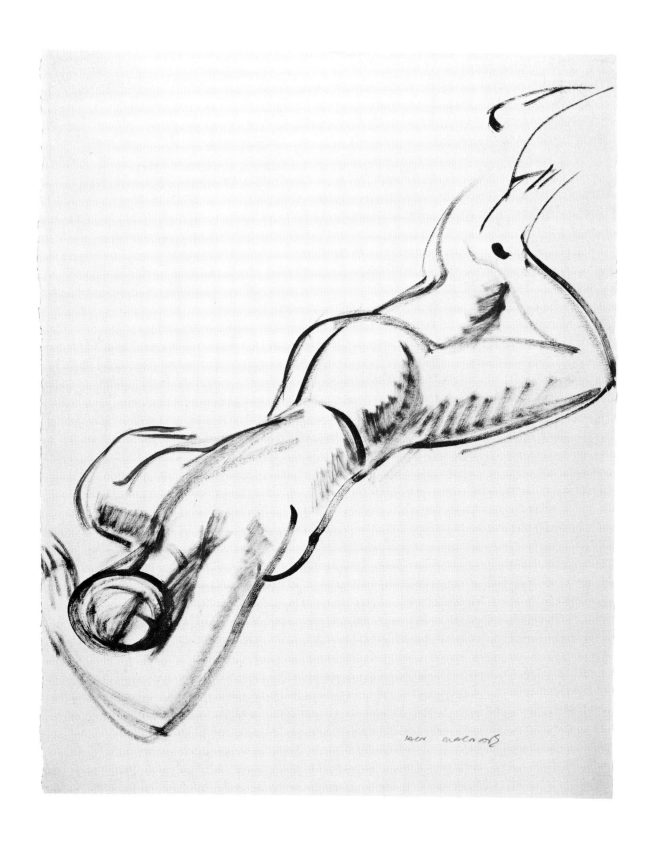

Figure 48 –   *Jane – sleeping*

Figure 49 —   *Jane —reclining*

6 - The teacher and organiser

33 Warwick Square, London, S.W.1. Iain's home, became famous in art, dancing and teaching. The building was large and rambling and appeared from the outside to have an ecclesiastical character and it was possibly an early coaching inn. It was also next door to the Church of the Square. By the time the book is published, however, the developers and town planners will have moved in for a large scale redevelopment of the area. The house commanded two addresses, as it had two entrances leading into two streets, one into Warwick Square and the other into Cambridge Street. In Cambridge Street almost opposite at No. 116 is the house where Aubery Beardsley lived and worked from 1872-1898. Previous to this move Iain lived at 5 Pembroke Walk Studios, Kensington, W.8.

Iain took over 33 Warwick Square in 1925, when he married Helen Mary Tench, a famous dancer and dance instructress. She was always an energetic and entertaining hostess to all his friends and guests. Her School of Dancing was conducted at 33 Warwick Square. Her professional name is Helen Wingrave, F.I.S.T.D., and she too has published books on dancing and is one of the leading English authorities on National Character Dancing. Like Iain, her art takes her into many countries. Iain grew very fond of Pimlico, it was quiet, and he had a small but walled in garden, which gave him the privacy that he valued so much. There are two wood engravings in which his back garden formed the subject. "The Mews at Night" 1954, which is a study based upon a street lighting scheme and "London Mews" (33 Warwick Square) 1952, *Fig.15,* which is a daylighting composition of architecture, perspective and foliage. He was very fond of the centre bed of hydrangeas. The bay tree in the tub is a typical London symbol of the small garden which appears in both engravings. What appears to be glass doors under the stairway is a very small greenhouse, which was always packed with a wide variety of plants and flowers.

Although the building was old and rambling it was endlessly fascinating inside. The acoustics were marvellous, dancing, art, conversation and privacy could all be taking place at the same time. There were enough bricks, stone and timber used in the structure to absorb and reflect the sound adequately. The same cannot be said of many buildings today. All the ceilings were high, thereby creating the right space relationships with people, and there was adequate daylight with privacy. All these architectural qualities are vital if city dwellers are to enjoy living, yet today these precious qualities are all being sacrificed in the name of economy, false or otherwise. His studio was L shaped in plan, with one door leading into his house and another into the Grosvenor School of Art. The tall French window doors opened on to the garden. In the studio the ceiling was very high and decorated with an Italian ceiling painting. The proportions of the studio were large and there is no doubt that this environment had a big influence on his work and the scale of the work. To have both the schools, studio and house in one building was a marvelleous arrangement for an artist, especially in relation to time saving and for production and entertaining. Many meetings of artists took place in this studio, and during the last six or seven years of his life the Society of Wood Engravers and Relief Printers always used to meet there. This society in its early days used always to meet in members studios. Now of course due to the cost of living, so many artists have to live well out of town.

In the world of print, teachers fall into two clearly defined groups. There is the print maker who is professional to the last degree, expressively cool, adequate pictorially and technically brilliant. This print maker is always a pace setter in teaching technique. Then there is the creative artist print maker, aesthetically experimental, expressively exciting pictorially, but in technical proficiency sometimes less than the former. The latter in form and development is however always in the end the more significant. Technique must always be the servant of form development, and its expression. Today we are in danger of confusing sheer technical brilliance with art as such. But in the world of print the creative and technical teacher will always acknowledge the contribution of the other. Because technique must serve form, most of the great print artists are either significant painters or sculptors. Both Iain and John Buckland Wright have said that it is important for an engraver to be a painter or sculptor, and Anthony Gross has said the same thing to his students at the Slade.

In teaching Iain embodied not only the painter and draughtsman, but the print maker as well wrapped into one. In print he was also an exponent of etching, lino-cut and lithography. His versatility was very unusual and these numerous means of expression are all basic, with the unifying element being draughtsmanship. Today it is fashionable to underwrite the value of draughtsmanship, but then it is after all a passport to many worlds. Even in teaching today the bottom seems to have fallen out of the ship, navigation is aimless in the name of freedom and the wayward draughts blow the crippled craft farther and farther off course. It is by no means unusual today to hear students say that drawing and life drawing is old hat. Perhaps the "Draughtsman" ship must go to the port of "Oblivion", before a new crew are found to steer her back on course again, to explore afresh the yet uncharted fields of form. In the cycle of time many things have to be lost, before they can be rediscovered.

Artists are generally good teachers, because they are committed men and women. Their professional commitment and the support of their actual production and experience is their authority. A person who studies art just to take up teaching can never have this authority, which is so vital in professional training. Also all students know the answer in the case of each master within the first three weeks of contact. And the student in that time will decide either privately or publicly whether so and so, has it or not. If he or she has not got it, it will be a case of two things are missing, experience and the ability to produce the expected results. These people can however, and do, very good work and make successful careers training younger students in schools preparing them for A and O level examinations in readiness for the final professional training. Any school at any time is only as good or bad as the teaching staff it can command. Naturally a good teaching team must be supported by good administration.

During my student days there were those whom I revered then and now and there were also those to whom I could not bear to be even near. Much later on in life, when I too started teaching architecture students the art that they required, I experienced the same thing, the student deciding whether you were an artist or not, within the first three weeks of contact. It is the judgement of Pontius Pilate, which in architecture has to be lived with for five years. But Iain started making this kind of judgement quite early in fact at school, when he told his art master at the Merchiston School that his drawing, teaching of the subject and approach was quite wrong. But Iain admitted to me that the master then was right when he told the immature Iain, to "get out". Which he did, smartly.

There is an ironical situation here in that thousands of good art masters are wanted in all our secondary and comprehensive schools all over the country. Also virtually all students want to be taught drawing by a draughtsman. However much money may be expended on training teachers, there is no hope of the wide gap ever being closed. It is difficult enough to produce sufficient good draughtsmen, who can teach, to man all the professional schools. The teaching of the subject is so personal that it calls for some of the qualities of an actor, especially if on a particular session, one is feeling like anything other than having to produce a good drawing, yet alone on a students drawing board. Yet one dare not sit on the students donkey and produce a bad or clumsy demonstration.

In teaching at the professional level it is sad to see the faces of aspiring eighteen year old students, starting their final technical training course, bolstered by their A levels in art, then being told to forget that they ever had such things, over and above the fact that these were required qualifications for them to be on the course at all. But having said that, the responsibility to produce the goods or results is without fail. If a failure does occur, then the student has been seriously confused and the lecturer should not teach above A or O level. Both lecturer and student are on trial, and a very close understanding and appreciation must grow freely between them. This kind of relationship is becoming yearly more difficult to maintain, due to the large number of students, the requirements of the examination and tuition structure of the current Diploma in Art and Design, which in Iain's time was the National Diploma of Design. The whole structure of teaching on these courses is broken down and segmented into specialisations into which the art staff are designed to fit. We must however grant that this is the only way in which the many can be catered for. But if, and heaven forbid, a potential student has a simple desire and the talent to become an artist as such, then he or she is due to be seriously frustrated by the Dip.A.D. examination structure and system. Should he or she wish to become a painter, sculptor or engraver then an equal frustration arises. The Dip.A.D. structure is built around the idea that an artist must be better educated, his training must be biased to the application of jobs, and that in art he must be a Jack of all trades, tasting all but mastering none. When a student has completed the Dip.A.D. course, can he really say that he is in any way qualified as an artist, to produce painting, sculpture or engraving? All are fundamental disciplines, each demanding complete commitment.

My student days were spent firstly at Camberwell School of Art, then at the Anglo French Art Centre and on to the Slade School of Fine Art and the course ran for four years, just studying painting and engraving. I wanted to become proficient at both and I certainly, at that time, never gave a thought about fitting myself for a job, or for that matter being better educated in the strict meaning of the term. Neither at that time would I have listened to any one trying to save my soul. Also at this point in time I have no regrets, but thanks for a Government grant and that I was not forced to go through such a system as the present Dip.A.D. My experience as a student in the private school materialised at the Anglo French Art Centre, which was directed by the painter Rozlar Green. The building used to be the older St. Johns Wood Art School. The Anglo French Art Centre was run on the basis of an "Academy Libre", where the fundamental disciplines of painting, sculpture and engraving only were taught and practised. The staff were very carefully chosen and much of the critical work and assessment was done by visiting French artists, such as Leger, Lorjo, Dom Rombert and the European art critic Nestra Giacometti and other English residents such as Oskar Kokoschka, Henry Moore, Basil Taylor and the late Eric Newton. A student could not wish for a better spectrum of the art of his time than this. This is of course the kind of training that most yearn for, but which cannot be made available to everyone. Yet despite its common sense, high ideals and achievements the school went bankrupt and from there I went to the Slade.

This is establishing a case and a plea for personal tuition, and quite logically on the free choice of master and student relationship, which for art is what is referred to as the apprentice system of education. This system has worked satisfactorily for centuries of artists, and is commonly referred to as professional training. In my case and in many others it worked well, and they were some of the most exciting years of my life. Yet in Universities this is not educating a person, and professional training must as such be kept outside. Then those responsible for the new policy had the brief to build the Dip.A.D. up to degree status, so that the art student would thereby become more employable, better educated for what, and not a better artist or designer in any respect.

It would appear now that we may be arriving at a point where it will be opportune for the rebirth of the private school once again. When things go badly wrong in art, then the all important private school becomes a safety valve.

Iain had the distinction of running a private art school successfully for a longer period than any one else. This was the Grosvenor School of Modern Art at 33 Warwick Square, which he ran for fifteen years. There was no beating about the bush with Iain, it was simply that there were people who wanted professional training, based upon the principles which were known to work, namely of the apprentice system and individual instruction. He gathered a sympathetic staff together and got on with the job.

Some students need more training than others, so that students at the Grosvenor could book in for periods as long as they wished. Possibly this idea also arose from his own experience. His professional training only occupied a short period following the first Great War in which he suffered grave injuries.

Iain studied art for six weeks at the Glasgow School of Art, 1917 and later in Paris. After the Glasgow School session he was again ordered back to the hospital bed where he stayed for another year. On being released he had another burst of study and this period was ended in a similar manner. The first Great War over, he went as a student to Heatherley's School of Art in London, and within six months was, at the Principal's invitation, (discreetly keeping dark his brief experience, and trusting to his lucky star and native wit to pull him through) was persuaded to be appointed joint principal. He stayed six years and left to found his own school. His co-principal at Heatherley's was Henry Massey and the partnership was dissolved in 1925 when he founded his own school at 33 Warwick Square. Also in that year he had to return to hospital, and for three months was packed in ice. But despite these set backs the Grosvenor School of Modern Art flourished until it was forced to close in 1940 on the outbreak of the Second World War starting in 1939. During this time a number of highly successful artists were produced, and it appears that he was particularly successful with the wood engravers. In fact his teaching contribution to the development of wood engraving was considerable, and his influence was far reaching.

We find one of his earliest teaching successes at the Westminster School of Art, one of the first L.C.C. Schools to teach abstract art during the 1930's under the dynamic leadership of a determined Principal, Kirkland Jamieson who accepted the changing future as inevitable and began the study of art as an abstract creative thought process. Kirkland Jamieson, an artist of no mean power gathered around him a talented and dynamic staff comprising such men of vision as Bernard Meninsky, Mark Gertler, Blair Hughes Stanton, Ernest Fedarb, Clifford Webb and Tom Chadwick. Of that time Ernest Fedarb said "It was much more revolutionary and far more difficult to make the first break with the rigours and traditions of drawing from life and the antique cast. Today we have become so used to change and take the revolution for granted regardless as to whether the quality is running up or down."

Tom Chadwick was the youngest member of the staff and he was trained as an artist and wood engraver by Iain at the Grosvenor School of Modern Art. Iain always spoke of Tom Chadwick as a brilliant creative artist in engraving. He also spoke of him as his finest pupil. Whilst discussing Tom Chadwick recently with Ernest Fedarb he described him as a brilliant engraver with a very high potential. Guy Malet has also described him to me as of exceptional quality. Tom Chadwick was very young to hold his first teaching post at the Westminster School and indeed virtually every professional opinion expressed on him in the press unanimously agreed on his brilliance and high potential for the future. In the few works that I have seen of his, I too rate him as high as all the opinions quoted. Naturally at his age there are not many works extant by him. For a short period a few works were published in magazines and a few exhibition reviews. He also exhibited a total of six works with the Society of Wood Engravers from 1932 to 1939. In January 1936 he had a notable success at Chicago with his wood engraving "The Introduction" and won the prize and medal awarded by the Committee on Prints of the Art Institute of Chicago, for the best print of the year shown at the 5th International Exhibition of Lithography and Wood Engraving. The exhibition comprised representative work from at least eighteen different countries. He was then twenty one years of age. He has engravings in the permanent collections of the British Museum, the North-ampton Art Gallery and the Chicago Gallery. In the July issue of the Studio, 1937, a short article was published on his work.

The short, but glorious trial of Tom Chadwick ends in the final sacrifice at the Battle of Alemain. During the last war he and his brother joined the Hussars and fought as tank crew in Lord Montgomery's "Desert Rat Campaign" in North Africa. Both brothers were killed in the battle. Tom Chadwick, risking everything, making the ultimate victory over self, attempted to recover the dead body of his brother and was shot while doing so. Ernest Fedarb who worked with him while teaching at the Westminster School said that his humanist values were remark-able and that he was completely open and extrovert in character. He was born in Yorkshire, a member of a well known Rochdale family, being a grandson of the late E.L. Chadwick, the former Castleton and Lancashire county cricketer.

In 1927, Guy Malet, R.B.A., a well known painter and wood engraver, joined the Grosvenor School of Modern Art where he was trained by Iain. From that time onwards they remained life long friends. Guy Malet commands an important position in the development of modern wood engraving, bringing to it a very sensitive talent and superb engraving skill. His engraving "Sark Girl" is possibly his most well known image. His is particularly masterly in producing the very rare silvery and shimmering greys, through the optical inefficiency of the eye's ability to differentiate an excess of visual information made available to it. A quality only found in front rank engraving.

In a brief appreciation by an old friend and a student, Guy Malet considers Iain as a teacher, to be an outstanding one. He says, "His advice was clear and incisive, and one invariably got the point he was making straight away, aand became keen to progress along the paths he suggested.

Iain's teaching had wisdom, reason and experience and was invariably imparted with the patience, charm and humour, so natural to him. His criticism and his lecturing was never dull or prosaic, and always conveyed something of interest and value.

Until I came under his guidance, I had seldom felt the same interest or assistance in studying, and often felt at a loss as to aim and direction in a field so wide and diverse as represented by art. But 'Mac' as he was known to so many, seemed to possess an uncanny, yet apparently effortless ability to draw a student out and to inspire keenness to progress.

There was no doctrinaire method insisted upon, each student being encouraged to 'find himself' and develop along his own lines, be it traditional or modern.

Whilst I was at the Grosvenor School of Art, which he founded, he initiated a class in wood engraving and persuaded me to join. Though I knew (and admired) his engravings, I had not regarded the craft as something I was myself even likely to practise. But I soon became fascinated in the use of the burin and gradually became for me a constant means of expression. Today, forty years later, I still practise it with pleasure.

Without the encouragement of Iain, I think that, like myself, many students of his would have missed much in their lives and outlook. Today, I miss him still, not only as a wise adviser and critic, but also as an old and very valued friend."

Gwenda Morgan was also one of Iain's star pupils, who since has also become a star performer in wood engraving. Wherever her engravings appear she is always stylistically consistent and immediately identifiable. It is a remarkable thing that in this century women are achieving master status in sculpture and engraving, far more so than in painting. Both these disciplines demand singleness of purpose and the ability to express ideas in mediums which cannot give immediate results. It may well be the severe strictures of these tough media that leads them to the straight and narrow road to success. Much of Gwenda Morgan's work is for books. Her flowing rhythms are unmistakable.

Gwenda Morgan in appreciation of Iain as a teacher has this to say, "He was a wonderful man and I have very happy memories of the times I spent at the Grosvenor School. I was not a full time student there. I used to go up to London each month for two nights so that I had three days at the School. A class that we all enjoyed very much was the composition class. Mac used to come in and set a subject and then leave us to work feverishly for one hour in any medium we liked. When he came back we propped our drawing boards against a row of chairs and he criticised our work. He always had a tremendous sense of humour and he was always encouraging. However bad a composition might be he was never anything but kind and helpful and I wish I could now remember all the interesting and witty tales that he could tell.

The wood engraving class was quite small, only about seven or eight of us while I was there and I remember that when Mac told new students what tools etc, to buy he used to add 'and a bottle of iodine'. He said it would be needed sooner or later.

Once a month in the evening there used to be a Sketch Club meeting and students' work was hung in the upstairs ball-room and Mac used to get a well known artist to come and criticise it. I remember one evening very well when Mark Gertler came. R.H. Wilinski came several times.

The things I chiefly remember about Mac are his great kindness, his sense of humour and his encouragement to the students."

Other pupils who later made their mark as good engravers were Alison and Winifred Mackenzie, Pauline Logan, Rachel Reckitt and William Kermode. The measure of a school is the quality of the students it turns out. For instance if a person is engaged in teaching, the thing that matters is results.

Teaching can take many forms at many levels of experience, especially ranging from youth to maturity. He was very practised in lecturing to adult audiences, opening exhibitions and giving criticisms to provincial art societies. He said of these occasions, "The amateur asks for professional criticism. If you give it them, you are in for one hell of a row. They really mean praise." He would however always set out to enjoy these occasions, and beforehand pray that his wit would flow freely. In June 1930 he was addressing the Clifton Arts Club in Bristol and said, "He thought Art Exhibitions would be better without catalogues. Pictures might then be judged on their merits, and not mentioned because so-and-so had painted them. But though neither title nor artist was mentioned, the price should be plainly stated." The same evening he said, "He did not think the artist was justified in considering other people at all in painting his pictures — it was for those who looked at his pictures to discover what the artist had to say to them." On the one hand he refuses to meet any form of commercial demand and, yet being the Scotsman that he was he made sure that the price was plainly stated. Many artists would quarrel with such a close and sharp relationship between art and selling, but for Iain there was a simple answer. If the work was of high quality people would want to own the work. I remember putting the point to him that a work may be of high quality but it might well take many years and many exhibitions for the twain to meet. Again his answer was a simple one, "Put the price up to cover the cost of keeping it, then if the purchaser retains it, he or she will make a profit and still be happy".

Iain was the visiting artist and prize adjudicator at the 1936 end of year function at St. John's Wood Art School. He said to the students, "The quaint suggestion that the ideal premises in which to instruct art students in painting from models were those in seven storeys. Such an idea originated from one of the leading French masters who, in order to impress upon his pupils the importance of relying upon their imagination and not being mere copyists of nature, used to pose the models on the top floor of a tall building and make the students complete their work in a studio on the ground floor, with the result that after they had made the first sketch from the model, they preferred to work it up from the imagination, rather than undergo the fatigue of running up and down fifty or sixty stairs every time they wished to refresh their memory." At that time a very important International Surrealist Exhibition was held at the New Burlington Galleries. This exhibition was on every student's mind. It was organised by Paul Eluard and the late E.L.T. Mesens, and Salvador Dali appeared at the private view in a diving suit. The public were outraged. This diving suit, with Dali in it proved to be one of the most outstanding press gimmicks of this century and the publicity was enormous. Surrealism officially ended in much the same way as did Cubism. When the leading exponents had worked it through, they broke their ranks and declared the movement as officially ended. It virtually started with the poets and ended with them. Although Surrealism is an important part of the imaginative life of art, painters cannot, and never have accepted the Surrealist anti-painting techniques that were used. Such a situation at the time must have been very confusing for the students. Iain continued to the students, "Speaking of the Surrealist Exhibition and what had been said of the state of mind which had prompted the composition of some of the works, I was much more interested in the pictorial reactions of these works, than in the artists' state of mind, which I feel they ought to keep to themselves." However typical of Iain, he dislikes Surrealism, but awarded three certificates to the then unknown student John Minton, one for a still life in oils, one for a Surrealist pen and ink study, and one for a striking theatre scene. He always retained a close interest in John Minton's career and development as a significant artist.

Iain also took part in one of the earliest television broadcast art education programmes in the very early days of experimental television and appeared on a programme on 3rd December 1937. The programme was devised as a series to demonstrate how different artists approach the same subject and it was entitled "Artists and their work". R.H. Wilenski, a well respected and lively art critic of his time, introduced three artists to the cameras: John Skeaping was introduced as a painter and sculptor of representational form, Iain Macnab as one who symbolised form and also worked in poster art (and he would always play the ball required for an occasion) and Amedee Ozenfant was described as a visitor from France who worked in the Cubist style (he became famous as a painter in this country much later). The programme was

produced by Mary Adams. By this time Ozenfant was already famous as a Cubist painter, and Le Corbusier the painter and now world famous as an architect, developed together the Purist Manifesto, which promulgated a very pure form of Cubism. This contributed to the eventual breakdown of Cubism. Also at that time Ozenfant had his own school, and while in London he spent a considerable amount of time with Iain.

Each artist on the programme was presented with a bowl of fruit and as all three were strongly individualistic, humour was provided by the amusing study in contrasts. Many of those who watched the broadcast were viewing the day's art for the first time. On looking back it is interesting to note that during the previous week's broadcasting Alexandra Palace had succeeded in the satisfactory reception of vision signals on board the Cunard-White Star liner, the Britannic, thirty miles out in the Channel and at least one hundred miles from Muswell Hill. This was seen then as a final blow to the theory of "optical" range.

The Britannic feat was however carried out as a scientific test by a private company. Telephotograms were also transmitted at this time to ships at seas as a visual message of greeting to the ship's crew. Now programmes are relayed by satellite to all parts of the world.

By this time Iain had produced several posters on travel mainly for British Railways. These were wood engravings blown up to poster size. Such posters do demonstrate the fact that wood engraving and its clarity of line and image could given the opportunity make a considerable impact on their production. But before this can happen again we must wait for more imagination to find its way, preferably into company publicity management. It is not much use relying upon advertising agents for this kind of imagination, because they must by contract produce what the customer or client demands.

In 1934 he also became involved in an imaginative venture which was conducted by Greenly's Ltd. the advertising agents for the National Building Society. Mr. F.E. Ball their managing director and Mr. David O'Connell the art director set out to sell to industry the idea of using our top line artists to sell the goods produced by industry. The scheme did get under way and the artists supported it. The inspiration had been fired off from the several examples of big industrial concerns such as Shell-Mex and the Underground Railways. These schemes had demonstrated that front rank artists have succeeded in interpreting commercial aims without restricting the artist. Mr. F.E. Ball did however make a sharp point when he said "You must remember that the firms mentioned have been particularly fortunate in having individuals inside their organisation who are capable of expressing their aims and in obtaining the sympathetic co-operation of the artist. I mean that they have J.L. Bedington and F. Pick. Very few firms happen to have such men within their walls." The support for this scheme was considerable. At the Royal Academy Banquet, the Prince of Wales stressed more than ever the need for co-operation between manufacturer and artist. Although the scheme at that time was only just launched, it is on looking back, interesting to see the artists who supported the scheme. They were John Armstrong, Mark Gertler, C.R.W. Nevinson, Walter Bayes, Charles Ginner, Ethelbert White, James Pryde, Anton Lock, Clare Leighton, Stephen Bone, Arnold Mason, Stephen Gooden, Robert D. Greenham, Iain Macnab, Gerald Moira, Leonard Squirrel, Graham Sutherland, Ernest Proctor and Bernard Meninsky. Each artist was selected as a specialist in his or her own sphere. An exhibition of these artists' first year's work was held in November 1934 at the Alpine Club, 23 Savile Row.

Iain's contribution to this scheme amounted to at least five wood engravings, designed to sell houses, detached and semi-detached, and these advertisements were published in the Sunday Express. Why did the scheme peter out? No one seems to know! Such schemes are always difficult to work on timing, budgets and the available personnel in both the Advertising Agencies and the companies who are their clients. The commercial artist is always in the studio on the premises, employed to produce anything the client wants at a moment's notice. I walked into a Baker Street Advertising Agency to see the Art Director, and when I arrived he was working on a drawing, looked tired and despondent. He said, "The client demands that the man I have drawn is laughing." To this I replied, "But the man is showing the back of his head." The Art Director said, "Yes, that is the problem, this was decreed by a different executive in the Company." I could not be bothered to find out if and how the Art Director resolved the matter.

In 1932 Iain's work in teaching led him to a fellowship in the Royal Society of Arts. The Society's purpose is "the encouragement of arts, manufacturers and commerce" and was founded in 1754. Its chief activities today, which are conducted from their house in John Adam Street, Adelphi, which it has occupied since 1774, are mainly educational and the encouragement of all levels of good industrial design; the operation of a nationally respected system of commercial examinations, the arrangement each year of expository lectures on topics of national importance; and the publication of the monthly Journal. The society has about 9,000 fellows distributed through the world and, as has been the case throughout its history, enjoys the support of prominent men and women in all walks of life. It is an independent, non-political organisation, holding by virtue of its wide interests and long record of service, a unique position among British institutions. The Royal Society of Arts held the very first public exhibition of contemporary art in this country in 1760 in the Great Room and it proved to be a great financial success. Apart from the highly important precedent which it sets, the exhibition also had the result of leading to the foundation in 1768 of the Royal Academy, which has been self supporting from the proceeds of its exhibitions ever since. The Society were also the orginators of the first international exhibition, the Great Exhibition of 1851. In 1852 it held the first public exhibition of photographs and within one month they had founded the Royal Photographic Society.

Among the more notable lectures given in the Society's famous and beautiful Lecture Hall may be mentioned Graham Bell's description of the telephone (1877), Hiram Maxim's account of the first flight in a heavier-than-air mechanically-propelled machine (1894), first reports by Marconi of some of his inventions (1901 and 1924) and Sir Howard Florey's classical account, with Sir Alexander Fleming in the Chair, of the discovery of penicillin (1944) and this record continues to the present time.

Among its many activities in promoting good industrial design, the Society's Council confers on outstanding British designers the exclusive distinction of "Royal Designer for Industry" (R.D.I.) the highest to be obtained in the field of industrial art. It can normally be held by not more than seventy designers at one time and applications for its award are not entertained. Enid Marx was the first woman to receive this award in 1942 and she is an engraver in wood and lino and a member of the Society of Wood Engravers and Relief Printers which she joined in 1955.

As an organiser of art Iain made an important contribution to London's art world. He spent much more time than most, fighting for fair play in art promotion, and opening doors to young talent. The larger body of his work was done through the London professional art societies. His main fields of operation and influence were as President of the Royal Institute of Oil Painters, the Honorary Auditor of the Royal Society of Painter Etchers and Engravers, as a permanent officer of the National Society and without office he ran the Society of Wood Engravers and Relief Printers for a long time. He also spent a lot of time defending the legal rights of artists and fighting legal art cases, which was done through his work as the Chairman of The Imperial Arts League. The legal work is secret and naturally unreportable material, but none the less real. He was elected Chairman in 1962 and continued in this office until he died. The Imperial Arts League is a body to whom artists can take any legal problem or case.

When considering artists from the point of view of organisation, they must be properly viewed as a full spectrum, the whole of which constitutes the art of our time. The full spectrum comprises the fundamental disciplines of painting, sculpture, engraving, drawing and all aspects of design. From these basic forms of expression further important branches arise such as the artist print maker, stained glass designers, illustrators, jewellery designers and so on. The need for promotion, and establishing contact with the public arises and the professional society has evolved as a means of achieving these ends. If the professional society functions properly it will exact standards for membership, and through the collective effort stage exhibitions, which would otherwise be beyond the scope of individual promotion. Societies have in the past and still do today, form themselves around a fundamental discipline such as painting or sculpture, and the public like their exhibitions this way. They can then go to view one discipline in concentration. Virtually all our exhibitions in industry are based upon this single principle. It is understandable that the public would suffer severe indigestion if all the disciplines were mixed. But there are those who would advocate such a move. Art societies are really extensions into modern life of the much older stystem of guilds. It is a case of the feathers of a bird stick together, rather than the birds of a feather flocking together. There are however a few societies where all the birds of a feather flock together, but their life is usually of much shorter duration. Societies also become pressure groups, some working for future change and others for reactionary ends and others for the status quo. As a result of pressure groups, societies sometimes break open and give rise to splinter groups demanding change. Some of these splinter groups have developed into important and dignified societies and very many more are gone and forgotten.

Whatever views may be held about art societies and their exhibitions, the fact remains that young and mid career artists must have a platform in the centre of London. Such a platform at the best of times is bound to be expensive. To make such a platform possible an art gallery with a lot of wall space must exist, its costs cleared and exhibitions must be mounted. Then it becomes the sensible thing for artists to join together to defray the costs to the individual. By these means it becomes possible for individuals in any part of the country to get some of their work shown in London. Without these societies new talent would be in a very sorry plight. Some would strike lucky purely by personal contact, but the majority would never see the light of day. To be unknown in the provinces is the same thing as being in a desert. In some parts of this country no art ever penetrates at all and this is the equivalent to being left behind on the moon.

The next point that arises is quality and in quality the values range from the unmeasurable best to the worst. John Buckland Wright once told me that the difference between London and Paris was that the best and worst in London were both less than in Paris. A more difficult commodity still is originality. Would you be able to recognise originality if you saw it for the first time and probably in a confused state as is always the case with the early works of an artist? You would be looking for something which you had not seen before, it would be a language, and as it had had no previous existence, then you would have no knowledge by which you could rightly determine it as new. From this point of view a person widely erudite in all the current languages and their history could certainly say with some authority that he knows of no previous parallel. But this person has only narrowed the field and is in the same position as the previous case of not knowing what the new will look like, he will not know what he is looking for. The next obstacle to discovering originality finds very common ground, in that it is only the rare individual who is able to overcome the deep psychological and virtually automatic rejection of the new which means change. This individual fear closes many eyes to new developments. In dealing with originality we are asking rather a tall question in that it took approximately thirty years after his death to begin to know what Cezanne was all about. It has taken almost the same time to arrive at a similar understanding of the meaning of the work of Paul Klee. But in the case of Cezanne and Klee, two recent extreme cases there were a few individuals who knew of the import before they died. However both these great artists achieved their first exhibitions through the societies and salons of their own countries. The same applies equally to this country. In the majority of cases famous names begin around the age of forty to fifty years, preceded by anything from twenty to thirty years work in the societies.

Many artists when they become successful forget about the others and especially those of younger age groups who still have their way to make. It is also only too well known that many professional artists have a closed mind to change, unless it is their own work, and resent the challenge of change which is represented by others. One sees this at work on selection committees where far too often they will vote only on works of their own kind. From this a selection principle arises..If you cannot change an individual, and individuals are all different, then it is important to change the individuals to judiciously change the collective result of the voting, which is a much better principle. There are however two more requirements, firstly the best number is an odd number and eleven has been found by experience to be the best for a large society. Secondly no selection committee should ever be repeated without some change. The opposite to this was carried out in Canada a few years ago. One artist was asked to select the works for a large exhibition and he selected three works only. This system has not caught on. I worked for many years with Iain on selection committees. On such an occasion in a pub I questioned him on the selection committee system. Iain's reply was "In my time many systems and variants have been tried, but you always come back to the eleven system. It is the system which so far has the fewest number of faults, and however good your committee may be there will always be some accident. The most important thing is of course a different committee each time. This does ensure that the same mistakes are not repeated."

My long friendship with Iain was always a happy one, but for him it was not always as comfortable as it might have been, I was apt at times to quite innocently involve him with the defence of principles. He was however training me for this kind of work and as a student I could not test his wisdom unless we became involved in an affair. Such an occasion arose in painting soon after Iain had been elected President of the Royal Institute of Oil Painters. At the 1960 selection committee of the R.O.I. three large abstract paintings came up, which were very adventurous and powerful works by a young unknown artist. A most unusual feature of these paintings was that they were painted in metallic pigments of copper, bronze and aluminium. However on selection committees there is a long standing code of behaviour, which requires that you exercise your voting powers and keep quiet for the rest of the time. All of these works were voted out. I then rose to my feet, furious and puffed out my chest and roared "Mr. Chairman, I demand to have these works returned for another vote." Bill Adams my senior in years and membership jumps to his feet waving his arms and declares "We are not having that stuff here, its not even paint. This is the Royal Institute of Oil Painters and I stress oil." Immediately I replied "Bill Adams has said that we are oil painters. He is of course right, but oil is only a medium, so he can have no objection to pigment." Iain responded to the clash with an instant reply. "Albert is right, we do only represent a medium and the medium used is oil. Bring the pictures back and vote again." All three paintings then received all the votes except for Bill Adams. These three previously rejected paintings all had to be hung in the exhibition, there were even no doubtfuls. For me however this was a good job of work done, but another thought was lingering in my mind. It was the tantalising fact that at all exhibitions, if all the works were passed in front of the same jury twice, there would be two very different results. Having committed the unforgivable sin of breaking up a sacred selection committee, I learned another lesson, which was if you do this sort of thing, then be absolutely sure of your guns and be prepared to resign if beaten. But when you do it for a sound cause the disturbance must be big and loud enough. To fluff it would be unforgivable.

Artists have many problems in living and working together as groups or in societies. To be an artist, every facet of the personality must be readable. Love and hate, intellect and emotion, and art and craft must go hand in hand with pride and prejudice. Prejudice will arise from firmly held opinions, beliefs, faiths and delusions and the individual will not always be aware of all the ingredients contributing to the whole. But prejudice can be difficult, especially where other people are concerned. It takes the form of adverse judgments in which hostility and ignorance play a major role and the person in question is often, blissfully unaware of the fact. No one is exempt from prejudice of some kind or degree and the condition is universal.

Most artists however want and are prepared to fight for freedom of expression. Freedom of speech and individual freedom to be fostered and worked out through democratic means and government. Yet all these freedoms lead to political anarchy. Anarchy in art is inevitable and in itself ensures change. People cannot help making mistakes and change saves them from a worse fate.

The strongest prejudice in art arises from the aesthetic and craft development and here each artist has a very personal stake to defend. Each artist knows that it takes a life time's work to build up a personality and due to the length of the time factor, must become at some time either outdated, outmoded or taboo, and this usually happens when the artist is at his peak. In this kind of change overtaking an artist, strong resentment will arise as a result of professional prejudice. This leads many senior artists into trying to influence various art groups and societies to fit their own ends and images. But this manoeuvre is not by any means confined to art societies, it often happens with artists who are fashionable working as jury on official exhibitions. These prejudices set up the permanent cycle conflict of the younger generation's opposition to the older generation. And the younger generation are often confounded when told, when they become successful professionally, they will in their turn also be the buttress for the generation to follow. On the question of prejudice Iain said, "The best way to overcome prejudice was to take up teaching. It makes you come out of it more humble. Sooner or later you will meet the student who will show you a clean pair of heels." I was able to test Iain with the older versus the younger in a Pygmalion choice while hanging an exhibition. At the end there was a place left for one more work. Wishing to give him a choice for a final decision I gave him two works of virtually equal quality, and both suitable on size and shape, but one work by a young unknown and an unknown of the mature generation. Iain's reply was "Hang the young person's work, the older one has probably had far more opportunities."

Not all artists are happy about numbers and the inevitable competition for a bright place in life. Some believe art to be non-competitive and support "the more the merrier", and others so professionally prejudiced cannot bear any one else in the field but them, and it is nothing uncommon to be subjected to a diatribe aimed at convincing the listener that the artist speaking is the only one that matters. There are many cases of famous artists who, when in company are unbearable bores, yet their publicity image can be quite the reverse. These cases often arise from the need for conceit to bolster the essential need for unquestioned self confidence, and for this to be deeply rooted in firmly held but prejudiced beliefs calls for some measure of forbearance on the observer's part. It is work which must be judged for its intrinsic value. But this kind of artist is in most cases quite unsuitable for working in a committee for the common good. His value as a decoration is however very real. There are other artists quite the opposite, enviably self effacing, soothingly relaxed, charming conversationalists, brilliant exponents of a sensitive vision and would willingly allow the world to tread on them. Obviously these are inefficient where business management is concerned. Multiply all these types of artist and the whole will produce only a very few personalities, strong enough to be respected by many and realistic enough to organise and run the business of a society. Equally these artists must be significant within the profession, otherwise they carry no authority. Iain's summing up of his experience in this field pin pointed the essential weakness of artists as organisers and he said, "They cannot add up a row of figures correctly and they cannot organise themselves, yet alone others." He also said and believed that the future of all the London Art Societies rested on the future formation of a Federation where all the management of the Societies could be done by a central and professional management body.

In the Societies' politics, race and colour problems would at times rear its head. On many occasions I have seen Iain cut through these issues, on the spot in a sharp surgical manner. His views on race and colour discrimination and apartheid were always clear and concisely expressed. As clear and concise as his line in his drawing. He would not tolerate discrimination anywhere and least of all in art. However intensely he was irritated on various occasions from those of other nationalities he always maintained the political principle of no discrimination. He visited Kenya in 1957 and there met the wood engraver Sybella Stiles, who at that time, together with friends was opposing the "whites only" decision, which was ruling the Kenya Arts and Crafts Society. His advice was sought and he said "They were quite mad to make it Europeans only". This madness does show in white African art. Stylistically they do not seem to know whether they are ducks or geese. The most pathetic manifestations of the white dilemma is the white artist adopting the forms of the indigenous races. This mongrel art of the white minority can only become more mongrel.

The defence of the individual is the ultimate sanity of man, for Iain was no song to be just sung to an audience, it was to be practised at all times. He carried out these concepts in all the exhibitions that he organised. As there was more built in safety for the individual in the committee of eleven rather than five, so there was safety in more Societies, more critics, journals, galleries and dealers and good work would then stand a better chance of survival.

It was this life long ideal which he was quick to see in the concept of a Federation of British Artists, and when the time came to turn the Federation into a reality he was ready and took positive action. The difference between a Federation and a Royal Academy is a fundamental one in that an Academy is a relatively closed society, centered around a very limited number of associates. The exhibition committees, which change each year are always drawn from the restricted group of associates. This means that the associates can be selective, which they are and at the same time pull the blinds down on some artists. Such prejudgements are not necessarily carried out at meetings, but sent round on the grape vine. Such undesirable closed shop competition cannot take place in a Federation, for the simple reason that the Federation will mount a continuous series of exhibitions through the year, with a large number of continuously changing selection committees. The Royal Academy only stages one open exhibition per year. A Federation gives a much greater safeguard for real talent to see daylight.

The idea of the London Art Societies federating for their future benefit was discussed as far back as 1939. It was also a well known fact that individual Societies had very bad administration. The idea of a central organisation for their administration was a good one and inevitable for their survival. Equally important was the need for these Societies to be able to speak with one voice and plan ahead and safeguard their future.

In 1958 it had been realised that a number of London Art Societies would be faced with the termination of their leases and two major Art Galleries were then known to be doomed. The first to go was the Royal Institute Galleries, 195 Piccadilly, which was built by the Royal Institute in 1880. A second Gallery to close in 1971 was the Royal Society of British Artists, who built their Gallery in 1825 at 6½ Suffolk Street, Pall Mall East. At this time London was being redesigned by John Nash. He was designing buildings from Regents Park to Carlton House Terrace with Regent Street and Suffolk Street in between. Nash designed a novel roof structure for 6½ Suffolk Street but in 1885 the iron work gave way. At first there was a great controversy with Nash, when the Home Secretary (Sir Robert Peel) was consulted in view of his responsibility for the public safety. Nash reconstructed the roof after many delays.

These Gallery closures were early moves and consequences of a major redevelopment and Town Planning for London's West End and Covent Garden areas. In order to meet these eventualities and to provide adequate and modern Galleries and facilities for exhibitions it was suggested that certain senior Art Societies should agree to form a Federation, which could negotiate on their behalf, and also act as a central organisation for the administration of the Societies. A preliminary meeting of the Societies was held at the Arts Club in Dover Street on the 26th February 1959, when a "Pilot Committee" was formed. Those present at the meeting were Edward I. Halliday, President of the Royal Society of British Artists, Sir James Gunn then President of the Royal Society of Portrait Painters, Cosmo Clark of the New English Art Club, Lord Pearce of the R.B.A. and Maurice Bradshaw. Maurice Bradshaw then secretary for several of the Societies set the lawyers to work to create a structure for a Federation of British Artists and he and Edward I. Halliday, together with Mr. Holroyd Chambers a distinguished surveyor, opened up personal negotiations with the Crown Commissioners. At the first meeting it was made plain that under no circumstances could they find their way to a further renewal of the lease as the whole area was destined for redevelopment.

The small committee at that time comprised Edward I. Halliday, Sir William Hutchinson and Maurice Bradshaw, the Secretary General of the Federation. This small committee's efforts resulted in the formation of the Federation of British Artists, which was incorporated as a Charity on the 13th February, 1961. It was not until March 12th 1965 at a meeting chaired by Lord Perth, the Chairman of the Crown Commissioners, that the Federation committee were told of the possible use as galleries of the so-called "Podium"— that is, the long one-storied doric-columned lower part of Carlton House Terrace, facing on the Mall. Apparently it was Lord Perth's idea to bring together at Carlton House Terrace, certain Art and Learned Societies and Associations then housed elsewhere and today the Institute of Contemporary Arts and the Royal Society (from Burlington House), both in Carlton House Terrace and the Town and Country Planning Association, the Civic Trust and others have joined the Federation of British Artists at 17 Carlton House Terrace.

Carlton House Terrace was built, as part of a larger design prepared by Nash, to cover north and south of St. James Park; a fitting termination to his grand Marylbone-Westminster thoroughfare. He wanted to link its two blocks with a domed fountain, using some of the old columns of Carlton House, but this was turned down. In 1834 the Duke of York's column was made the centerpiece. Nash designed St. James Park as it is today and to break up the straight lines of its canals he created an islanded lake.

Iain was a director of the Royal Institute Company which was the managing company of the Royal Institute Galleries, 195 Piccadilly. Around 1965 a red light began to shine on the horizon. In a few years' time the lease on the building was to run out and the future of these Galleries continuing in art was certain doom. On such a site the rent for the Galleries would be far and away beyond anything which the Royal Institute Societies would be able to meet. In due course he resigned his directorship of the Royal Institute Company. Then as President of the Royal Institute of Oil Painters he transferred the R.O.I. over to the Federation of British Artists. The last R.O.I. exhibition to be held in the Royal Institute Gallery took place in 1967. In the meantime he and I had transferred the Society of Wood Engravers and Relief Printers over to the Federation in 1966. Other Royal Institute Societies also moved into the Federation. Many people however regretted losing the Royal Institute Gallery. It was the most centrally situated Gallery in London. The moving of the Society of Wood Engravers and Relief Printers coincided with the Crafts Centre of Great Britain's move from its premises in Hay Hill to Earlam Street, Strand. This Society was always very unhappy in its attachment to the Crafts Centre. The Crafts Centre was very much a dominating interest of John Farleigh and the Society joined the Crafts Centre in 1948. In terms of management it was found that the difference between the craftsman and the artist was too wide.

Many changes in London's art world were afoot at that time. The Federation of British Artists' Gallery, 6½ Suffolk Street, was due to close and be returned to the Crown and the last exhibition to be held there was the National Society of Painters and Sculptors in February 1971. The timing and closing of these major Galleries eventually gave birth to the Federation as a going concern. The object of the Federation was not only to provide adequate and modern facilities for art, but other functions as well. Another important object was to reduce the cost of administration, and improve the efficiency by co-operation in the use of a properly run Secretariat. It also guaranteed a permanent home for the many professional London Societies. An organisation had to be set up where all views could be ventilated and considered and the four essential requirements were: firstly the artistic integrity of every society must be preserved and not interfered with by other societies holding other views. Such an event may sound like a dream, but it is true and it works. Secondly there is the requirement that members of all societies must have a voice. This too is a reality. Thirdly, the societies must elect their own Councils and Officers who would control the administration of each society. This is true democracy at work. The culmination point of much of Iain's work. Fourthly there is the requirement that societies must have a seat on the Presidents' Council. Such a seat may at times be hot and prickly. It can however be seen that authority is finally vested in the members of the societies. The Federation is managed by a Board of Governors which is controlled by a Council of Presidents, and representatives of all societies should serve on that Council. Also the Federation is self supporting and received no grant from public funds or private for that matter and all its activities are financed by the artists themselves and from fees paid by the organisations benefitting from the assistance and advice given by the staff of the Federation.

No. 17 Carlton House Terrace was redesigned internally by the architect Kenneth Peacock F.R.I.B.A., of the Louis de Soissons Partnership. When completed No. 17 was officially named as the Mall Galleries. The Crown had been very generous and in consideration of the surrender at 6½ Suffolk Street had agreed to grant a new lease of twenty one years at a rent of £5,000 per annum. A capital cost for providing the Galleries and other accommodation was upwards of £200,000 and this was also provided by the Crown and the Federation contributed a nominal sum of £10,000 towards the costs.

The lighting, by necessity, is totally artificial throughout and comprises a mixture of fluorescent and tungsten energy. The mixture is made necessary through the inadequacy of the colour rendering properties of the fluorescent lamps. Their red deficiency is thereby partly made up from the excess red emission of the tungsten lamps. It is a carefully considered specification and it works reasonably well. The design of the lamp groupings is not accurately worked out as there are overhead shadows cast from the frames on the most important walls. On viewing works in the Gallery the artists and the public are unable to make a daylight colour comparison.

The rates of the Galleries which are half the normal is a concession made to the Federation as a charity. An estimated total cost of administering the whole organisation was slightly over £30,000. The Federation now has a total membership of artists of between 1,000 and 1,500 covering the whole spectrum of art. No other organisation can claim such a full spectrum. The new Mall Galleries were opened in February 1971 with an exhibition by the Federation's senior society the Royal Society of British Artists and Her Majesty the Queen performed the opening ceremony.

Iain became a Governor of the Federation of British Artists in 1959. He lived long enough to nurse his dream of an art democracy, which really works into a living reality. His concepts of justice and fairness in art affairs had been built into the constitution of the Federation.

Although Iain lived, worked and flourished for the greater part of his life in the land of the Sassenachs, he remained a Scotsman true in wit, thought and feeling. His maxim was always live with a minimum number of rules. All the time he was running the affairs of the Society of Wood Engravers it was always "a minimum number of rules" and the society is still doing it. He was interested in everything that the Sassenach did and he would only adopt, at any time, the art from whence it came that would enrich his Scottish heritage and tradition. Any thought of such aesthetic developments as an international style, which had duly arrived was an anathema to him and meant an immediate sell out of his concepts of individuality, which for him was sacrosanct. He would argue and with some justification that it is even contrary to man's biological structure. To Iain, the individual was all important, and the ultimate safeguard against tyranny of all kinds. Individuality and change was man's only hope of sanity, in that he simply cannot avoid making mistakes.

For this defence of human sanity and for leaving the world richer than he found it, he was dearly loved. Only a few burins will be so guided into such eloquent form.

BIBLIOGRAPHY OF EVENTS

1890 . . . . . Born Iloilo in the Philippines. 21st October.

1894 . . . . . Arrived in Scotland and lived at Kilmacolm.

1911 . . . . . Studied chartered accountancy at Rattsy Brothers, Alexanda and France. Glasgow.

1914 . . . . . Volunteered for military service with the Highland Light Infantry.

1915 . . . . . Commissioned and gazetted to the 2nd battalion The Argyll and Sutherland Highlanders (the famous 93rd) and served as Divisional Machine Gun Officer in France.

1916 . . . . . Invalided out of the Army. Two years spent in hospital.

1917 . . . . . Studied at the Glasgow School of Art.

1918 . . . . . More time spent in hospital. Then studied at the Heatherley School of Art. London.

1919 . . . . Studied in Paris, then became Joint Principle of Heatherley School of Art.

1923 . . . . . Elected Associate of the Royal Society of Painter Etchers and Engravers.

1925 . . . . . Left Heatherley School of Art to found his own school The Grosvenor School of Modern Art at 33, Warwick Square, S.W.1. Another operation and a long session in hospital.

1927 . . . . . Exhibited first wood engraving.

1928 . . . . Visited Paris and worked at Julian's.

1930 . . . . Painted in the South of France. (Cawclaire).

1931 . . . . Painted in Corsica. (Calor).

1932 . . . . . Married Helen Mary Tench, known in the dancing profession as Helen Wingrave. Painted in Majorca. Invited to membership of the Society of Wood Engravers. Fellowship to the Royal Scoiety of Arts.

1934 . . . . . Took a sketching party to the Costa Brava. (Tossa).

1935 . . . . . Fellowship of the Royal Society of Painter Etchers and Engravers. Took a sketching party again to the Costa Brava. (Spain)

1936 . . . . . Painted in Spain. (Gerona and Castel del Sol.)

1937 . . . . . Television appearance with R.H. Wilenski.

1939 . . . . Painted in Cornwall. On outbreak of war joined the A.R.P. and had the basement of 33 Warwick Square turned into an Air Raid Wardens Post which was visited by the Queen on September 2nd.

1940 . . . . . Served as fire officer with the A.R.P. during the London Blitz. Closed the art school. Elected Hon: Sec: to the Royal Society of Painter Etchers and Engravers.

1941 . . . . . Joined the R.A.F. and trained and lectured in R.D.F.

1942 . . . . . Invalided out of the R.A.F. and spent nearly a year in the Middlesex Hospital.

1943 . . . . . Rejoined R.A.F. and served as adjutant in various stations.

1945 . . . . . Once more invalided out of the R.A.F., then painted in a small studio in Chelsea as 33 Warwick Square was taken over by the Westminster City Council as offices for the re-housing settlement and the big studios by the Church of the Holy Apostles as their Church had been destroyed by enemy action.

1946 . . . . . Regained possesion of 33 Warwick Square and rented part of the building to The Heatherley School of Art and became their Director of Art Studies.

1949 . . . . . Took a Sketching party to Corsica. (Calis).

1950 . . . . . Painted in Yugoslavia.

1952 . . . . . Hon: Auditor to the Royal Society of Painter Etchers and Engravers.

1953 . . . . . Relinquished post as Director of Art Studies at Heatherley School of Art.

1954 . . . . . Painted in Southern Spain. (Andalusia.)

1956 . . . . . Visited Kenya and mounted an exhibition in Nairobi.

1957 . . . . . Took a sketching party to Scotland. (Aberfoyle).

1958 . . . . . Took a sketching party to Austria. The matriculation of the Arms of Macnab of Barachastlain.

1959 . . . . . Took a sketching party to Spain. (Sitges.) Elected President of the Royal Institute of Oil Painters. Became a Govenor of the Federation of British Artists.

1960 . . . . Took a sketching party to Ibins.

1961 . . . . . Took a sketching party to Saxonia. Produced his last wood engraving "Fonda Bridge". Spain. Formation of the Federation of British Artists.

1962 . . . . . Stayed with his brother-in-law in San Rogue and staged an exhibition of his work in the Calpe Institute. Gibralta. Elected Chairman of the Imperial Arts League. 18th October.

1963 . . . . . Painted in Northern Spain. Calicia.

1964 . . . . . Painted in Minorca.

1965 . . . . . An operation and another session in hospital.

1966 . . . . . Transferred Society of Wood Engravers and Relief Printers to the Federation of British Artists.

1967 . . . . . Transferred the Royal Institute of Oil Painters to the Federation of British Artists. Died in St. Thomas's Hospital 24th December.

1969 . . . . . Memorial Exhibition of over 236 works in the F.B.A. Galleries. 6½ Suffolk Street. Pall Mall East. London, S.W.1.

1927 . . . . . Winter..17.8 x 22.8.cm. (1st exhibit at R.E.s.).
1927 . . . . . A Zeeland Port..25.0 x 20.0.cm.
1927 . . . . . La Lessive.
1927 . . . . . Veere Harbour..39.5 x 22.2.cm.
1928 . . . . . The Glass Bottle..24.1 x 20.2.cm.
1928 . . . . . The Canal. Annecy..11.4 x 17.7.cm.
1928 . . . . . Mont Blanc..10.0 x 19.0.cm (black-green ink).
1928 . . . . . The Mirror.
1928 . . . . . La Lacon.
1929 . . . . . Le Quai de Isle. Annecy..26.27 x 28.6.cm.
1929 . . . . . Le Coutar.
1929 . . . . . A Village in Savoy..10.1 x 15.2.cm.
1929 . . . . . Hillside. Savoy..10.1 x 15.2.cm.
1929 . . . . . Le Sporting Bar..15.2 x 10.1.cm.
1930 . . . . . Arles..25.4 x 19.8.cm.
1930 . . . . . The Waterfront. Calvi. Corsica..20.0 x 25.4.cm.
1930 . . . . . Landscape. Cassis..15.0 x 9.0.cm.
1930 . . . . . Sardine Fisherman..9.5 x 11.1.cm.
1930 . . . . . A Mediterranean Port..
1930 . . . . . Landscape near Cassis. 10.7 x 9.1.cm.
1931 . . . . . Corsican Landscape..25.4 x 20.3.cm.
1931 . . . . . Mill in the Cotswolds..
1932 . . . . . Illustrated Book. Nicht at Eenie. The Bairns Parnassus. 48 Wood Engravings.
1932 . . . . . Saint Paul du Var.
1932 . . . . . Deya. Majorca..20.2 x 24.8.cm.
1932 . . . . . Apple picking.
1932 . . . . . A Majorcan Village..24.1 x 20.2.cm.
1933 . . . . . Southern Landscape..24.8 x 18.7.cm.
1933 . . . . . Landscape. Majorca..16.3 x 20.2.cm.
1933 . . . . . Calvi. Corsica..
1933 . . . . . Cassis..14.7 x 9.6.cm.
1934 . . . . Conversation Piece..
1934 . . . . . Illustrated Book. Tam O Shanter. 13 Wood Engravings.
1934 . . . . . National Building Society. Advertising. 6 Wood Engravings
1935 . . . . . Spring Landscape. Tossa. Spain.
1935 . . . . . From a Fonda Window..20.2 x 25.4.cm. subsequently renamed
1936 . . . . . Majorcan Landscape..20.2 x 25.4.cm.
1936 . . . . . The Game of Cards.
1936 . . . . . Bathers..
1936 . . . . . Two Fat Ladies. Portofino..20.2 x 25.4.cm.
1936 . . . . . Las Lavanderas..17.3 x 12.7.cm.
1936 . . . . . Portofino.. 28.6 x 20.6.cm.
1936 . . . . Fishermen. Portofino..25.4 x 20.2.cm.
1937 . . . . . The Quayside. Whitby Harbour..24.1 x 28.8.cm.
1937 . . . . . L.N.E.R. Poster. The Quayside, Whitby Harbour, engraving size..49.6 x 60.2.cm.
1938 . . . . . Gr-r-r.. 8.2 x 12.7.cm.
1938 . . . . . David and Saul..8.2 x 6.4.cm.

1938 . . . . . Artemis and Hippolutos..8.2 x 12.7.cm.
1938 . . . . . Saint Paul..20.2 x 24.4.cm
1938 . . . . . Abt Vogler..8.6 x 12.7.cm.
1938 . . . . . Soloman..7.6 x 9.5.cm.
1938 . . . . . Mourning.
1938 . . . . . Illustrated Book. Robert Browning, Selected Poems. 16 Wood Engravings.
1938 . . . . . Fra Lippo Lippi.8.3 x 12.7.cm.
1938 . . . . . Drying Sails, Lake Garda..19.1 x 21.8.cm.
1938 . . . . . Canterbury Pilgrims..15.2 x 8.8.cm.
1939 . . . . . Nature Morte..22.2 x 26.4.cm.
1939 . . . . . The Sailors Farewell..12.4 x 21.8.cm.
1939 . . . . . The Haunted Olive Grove. 10.1 x 12.0.cm.
1941 . . . . . Snow on the Radnor Hills..17.8 x 22.8.cm.
1943 . . . . . The Ferry Boat Inn..
1947 . . . . . Summer Bouquet..25.3 x 20.2.cm.
1947 . . . . . Gathering Wood..15.4 x 16.8.cm.
1948 . . . . . Illustrated Book. The Sculptured Garland. 16 Wood Engravings.
1948 . . . . . Death of Artemidora..12.7 x 17.2.cm.
1948 . . . . . The Graces..10.1 x 15.2.cm.
1948 . . . . . Fishermen. Battersea Park..25.1 x 20.0.cm.
1948 . . . . . The Maidens Lament.
1949 . . . . . The Fallen Willow..22.8 x 15.1.cm.
1950 . . . . . The House Opposite..24.2 x 14.2cm.
1950 . . . . . Gossip. Corsica..22.8 x 16.5.cm.
1951 . . . . . Le Marche..20.2 x 12.7.cm.
1951 . . . . . Cornish Boat Yard.
1951 . . . . . Saturday Shopping.
1951 . . . . . The Brave Bull..20.2 x 13.0.cm.
1951 . . . . . Flower Sellers. Yugoslavia..20.2 x 12.4.cm.
1952 . . . . . London Mews..(33 Warwick Square.)..14.5 x 9.6.cm.
1952 . . . . . The Carol Singers..(Samson Press)..10.1 x 10.7.cm.
1952 . . . . . A Spanish Farm..14.1 x 10.1.cm.
1953 . . . . . The Three Washerwomen..25.0 x 15.2.cm.
1954 . . . . . Snow Scene. (33 Warwick Square). (semi-circular). 7.6 x 10.2.cm.
1954 . . . . . Mews at Night. (33 Warwick Square). 12.9 x 10.3.cm.
1955 . . . . . London Snow. (from 1 st floor, 33 Warwick Square viewing Gloucester Street.). 12.6 x 20.3.cm.
1957 . . . . . Picking Pyrethrum in the Aberdares. Kenya. 20.9 x 15.2.cm.
1959 . . . . . Portuguese Shipyard..20.9 x 15.2.cm.
1959 . . . . . Back Gardens. Lisbon..21.8 x 15.4.cm.
1960 . . . . . The Sail Loft..15.1 x 20.2.cm.
1960 . . . . . River in Spate..20.0 x 15.2.cm.
1960 . . . . . Waterlilies..20.2 x 15.2.cm.
1961 . . . . . Ronda Bridge. Spain..20.3 x 25.4.cm.

CHECK LIST OF ILLUSTRATED BOOKS

1932 . . . . . Nicht at Eenie. The Bairns Parnassus.
The Samson Press.
48 Wood Engravings. 9.50" x 7.00".
1934 . . . . . Tam O Shanter.
The Samson Press.
13 Wood Engravings. 9.00" x 6.00".
1938 . . . . . Selected Poems by Robert Browning.
Penguin Illustrated Classics.
Penguin Books Limited.
16 Wood Engravings. 7.00" x 4.50".
1948 . . . . . The Sculptured Garland. Lyrical Poems by
Walter Savage Lander.
The Dropmore Press.
16 Wood Engravings. 10.25" x 8.00".

1951 . . . . . Introduction to Woodstock.
The Samson Press.
14 Pen Drawings. 8.75" x 5.50".
1936 . . . . . Figure Drawing.
The Studio Limited.
London.
1938 . . . . . The Students Book of Wood Engraving.
Isaac Pitman.
London.

CHECK LIST OF ARTICLES PUBLISHED

1932 . . . . . The Artist... Lithography. Part I.
Vol. IV. No.4. December.
The Artist Publishing Company.
London.
1933 . . . . . The Artist... Part 2. Lithography.
Vol.IV. No.5. January.
1933 . . . . . The Artist... Lithograph. Part 3.
Vol.IV. No.6. February.
1933 . . . . . The Artist... Part 4.
Vol.V. No.I. March.
1933 . . . . . The Artist... Lithography. Part 5.
Vol.V. No.2. April.
1939 . . . . . The Studio... The artist's approach to figure drawing.
Vol.II. No.552. March.
The Studio Publishing Company.
London.
1946 . . . . . The Artist... Pictorial Composition.
Vol.19. No.I. March.
The Artist Publishing Company.
London.

1958 . . . . . The Artist... Draughtsmanship. Part I.
Vol.56. No.4. December.
1959 . . . . . The Artist... Draughtsmanship. Part 2.
Vol.56. No.5. January.
1959 . . . . . The Artist... Draughtsmanship. Part 3.
Vol.56. No.6. February.
1960 . . . . . The Artist... Wood Engraving — Its History and Techniques.
Vol.59. No.2 April.
1960 . . . . . The Artist... Wood Engraving — Its History and Techniques.
Vol.59. No.2. April
The Artist Publishing Company,
London.
1961 . . . . . The Artist... Problems of the amateur.
Vol.61. No.2 April.
1961 . . . . . The Artist... Problems of the Amateur.
Vol. 61. No.2. April.
The Artist Publishing Company.
London.

WOOD ENGRAVINGS IN PUBLIC COLLECTIONS

1930 . . . . . Royal Scottish Academy. Edinburgh.
1934 . . . . . City Art Gallery, Manchester.
1934 . . . . . Musec de Arte Moderne. Parquese la Cindadala. Barcelona.
1937 . . . . . Whitworth Art Gallery. Manchester.
1937 . . . . . City Art Gallery. Belfast.
1939 . . . . . British Museum. London.
1939 . . . . . Edinburgh Art Gallery. Edinburgh.
1939 . . . . . Municipal Art Gallery. Cork. Gibson Bequest.

1939 . . . . . National Gallery. Zacheta. Warsaw.
1939 . . . . . National Gallery of Moscow.
1969 . . . . . Ashmolean. Oxford.
1969 . . . . . Victoria and Albert Museum, London.
Rotterham Corporation Art Gallery.
National collections of Canada, Australia, New Zealand and other European Countries.

SELECTED BIBLIOGRAPHY

De quelques graveurs anglais. Mark Severin. Bulletin de la Classe Des Beaux-Arts Academic Royal de Belgique. Bruzelles. *1953.*

Etching and engraving. Techniques and the modern trend. John Buckland Wright. Studio Publications. London. *1953.*

A check list of book illustrations by John Buckland Wright. Personal memoir by Anthony Reid. Private Libraries Assoc: Pinner, Middx. *1970.*

Lepere. Lotz-Brissoneau. Exhibition Catalogues 1905 and 1908. Paris.

An introduction to a history of woodcut. 2. Vols. A.M. Hind. Dover Pub Inc. New York. *1935.*

The woodblock engravers. Kenneth Lindley. David and Charles. Newton Abbot. *1970.*

New life in wood engraving. John Farleigh. Impulse. No.13. p.27-29. Journal Press. London. *1960.*

The engraver ghosts of Fleet Street. Albert Garrett. Impulse. No.25. p.27-30. Journal Press. London. *1964.*

Wood engraving in modern English books. Catalogue foreword. Thomas Balston. National Book League. O.U.P. Great Britain. *1949.*

The wood engravings of Robert Gibbings. Edited by Patience Empson, Introduction by Thomas Balston. J.M. Dent. London. *1959.*

Society of wood engravers 1920. Catalogue foreword. Campbell Dodgson. Society of Wood Engravers. London. *1920.*

The wood cut. An annual. Article by Eric Gill. Herbert Furst. Vol.I.2.3 & 4. The Fleuron Press. London. *1927-30.*

Wood engraving. George E. Mackley. National Magazine Co.Ltd. London. *1948.*

Wood engraving. John R. Beedham. St. Dominics Press. Ditchling. *1920.*

A history of wood engraving. Douglas Percy Bliss. Dent. London. *1928.*

Wood cuts and some words. Edward Gordon Craig. Dent. London. *1924.*

Contemporary English woodcuts. Campbell Dodgson. Duckworth. London. *1922.*

Graven Image. John Farleigh. Macmillan. London. *1940.*

Notes on the wood engravings of Eric Ravilious. Robert Harling. Faber. London. *1946.*

Wood engravings of the 1930's. Clare Leighton. The Studio. London. *1936.*

Wood cuts and wood engraving. Noel Rooke. Print Collectors Club. Royal Society of Painter Etchers and Engravers. London. *1926.*

Wood engraving since 1890. Bernard Sleight. Isaac Pitman. London. *1932.*

The engraved work of Eric Gill. John Physick. Victoria and Albert Museum. London. *1963.*

Woodcut, wood engraving. Imre Reiner. Publix Pub Co. London. *1947.*

The wood engraving of Joan Hassall. Ruari McLean. O.U.P. London

About prints. S.W. Hayter. O.U.P. London. *1962.*

New ways of gravure. S.W. Hayter. Routledge and Kegan Paul. Ltd. London. *1949.*

Wood engraving. Thomas Bewick. Dufour Editions Inc. Chester Springs. P.A.

Wood engravings of Gwendola Raverat. Reynolds Stone. Boston Books. Boston. Mass.

English wood engraving. Thomas Balston. Art and Technics. London. *1951.*

Edward Gordon Craig designs for the theatre. Janet Leeper. Penguin Books. London. *1948.*

The adventures of the black girl in search for God. Illustrated John Farleigh. George Bernard Shaw. Constable. London. *1932.*

Thomas Bewick. Graham Reynolds. Art and Technics. London. *1950.*

Robert Gibbings. Thomas Balston. Art and Technics. London. *1949.*

Eric Gill. Douglas Cleverdon, Art and Technics. London. *1951.*

Engraving on wood. John Farleigh. Dryad Press. Leicester. *1954.*

Your wood engraving. Mark F. Severin. Sylvan Press. London. *1953.*

Wood cuts and wood engraving. John R. Biggs. Blandford Press. London. *1958.*

Wood engravings by Thomas Bewick. John Rayner. Penguin Books. London. *1947.*

Thomas Bewick. Montague Weekly. O.U.P. London. *1953.*

Thomas Bewick and his pupils. Austin Dobson. Chatto and Windus. London. *1889.*

Memoir of Thomas Bewick. Thomas Bewick. John Lane. The Bodley Head. London. *1924.*

A manual of instruction in the art of wood engraving. S.E. Fuller. Joseph Watson. Boston. *1867.*

How I make wood cuts and wood engraving. Hans Alexander Mueller. American Artists Group Inc. New York. *1945.*

The art of wood engraving. Francis M. Reynolds. B.E. Hale. New York. *1879.*

Wood engraving since 1890. A Practitioner. Pitman. London. *1932.*

Blakes illustrations for Thornton's Virgil. Geoffrey Keynes. The Nonesuch Press. London. *1937.*

A history of wood engraving in America. W.J. Linton. George Bell and Sons. London. *1882.*

Engravings on wood. W.M. Laffan. Society of American Wood Engravers. Harper and Bros. New York. *1887.*

Wood engraving and wood engravers. Hiram Campbell Merrill. Society of Printers of Boston. Boston. *1937.*

The new wood cut. Malcolm Salaman. The Studio. London. *1930.*

The art of the American wood engraver. Philip Gilbert Hamerton. Scribner's Sons. New York. *1894.*

American wood cuts and engravings. Lawrence C. Wroth and Marion. W. Adams. John Carter Brown Library. Providence. *1944.*

On space and time in art (wood engraving). Albert Garrett. Leonardo. Vol.5. No.4. Oxford. *1972.*

Engraved bookplates 1950 to '70. Mark Severin and Anthony Reid. Private Libraries Association. Pinner. Middlesex. *1972.*